WALKING in YORKSHIRE

AIRE VALLEY
& BRONTE COUNTRY

HILLSIDE GUIDES - ACROSS THE NORTH

Yorkshire River Photobooks
- JOURNEY OF THE AIRE
- JOURNEY OF THE WHARFE

Walking in Yorkshire - North/East
- NORTH YORK MOORS South/West
- NORTH YORK MOORS North/East
- YORKSHIRE WOLDS
- HOWARDIAN HILLS & VALE OF YORK

Walking in Yorkshire - West/South
- AIRE VALLEY & BRONTE COUNTRY
- SOUTH YORKSHIRE

Walking in Yorkshire - Yorkshire Dales
- East: NIDDERDALE & RIPON
- West: THREE PEAKS & HOWGILL FELLS
- South: WHARFEDALE & MALHAM
- North: WENSLEYDALE & SWALEDALE

Circular Walks - Lancashire/North West
- BOWLAND
- PENDLE & RIBBLE
- ARNSIDE & SILVERDALE
- LUNESDALE

Circular Walks - North Pennines
- EDEN VALLEY
- ALSTON & ALLENDALE

Long Distance Walks
- COAST TO COAST WALK
- DALES WAY
- CUMBRIA WAY
- PENDLE WAY
- CALDERDALE WAY

Hillwalking - Lake District
- LAKELAND FELLS - SOUTH
- LAKELAND FELLS - EAST
- LAKELAND FELLS - NORTH
- LAKELAND FELLS - WEST

Short Scenic Walks - Yorkshire Dales
- UPPER WHARFEDALE
- LOWER WHARFEDALE
- INGLETON/WESTERN DALES
- RIBBLESDALE
- MALHAMDALE
- SWALEDALE
- NIDDERDALE
- UPPER WENSLEYDALE
- LOWER WENSLEYDALE
- SEDBERGH/DENTDALE

Short Scenic Walks - Yorkshire & Lancashire
- HARROGATE/KNARESBOROUGH
- ILKLEY/WASHBURN VALLEY
- AIRE VALLEY
- HAWORTH
- HEBDEN BRIDGE
- AROUND PENDLE
- RIBBLE VALLEY
- BOWLAND

*Send for a detailed current catalogue and price list
and also visit www.hillsidepublications.co.uk*

WALKING in YORKSHIRE

AIRE VALLEY
& BRONTE COUNTRY

Paul Hannon

Hillside

HILLSIDE PUBLICATIONS

2 New School Lane
Cullingworth
Bradford
West Yorkshire
BD13 5DA

First published 2018

© Paul Hannon 2018   ISBN 978-1-907626-23-4

Cover illustrations: Goit Stock; Penistone Hill, Haworth
Back cover: Five Rise Locks; Page One: Earl Crag, Cowling
Page Three: Farnhill Moor; Above: Saltaire; Opposite: Haworth church
(Paul Hannon/Yorkshire Photo Library)

The sketch maps are based on 1947 Ordnance Survey One-Inch maps

Printed in China on behalf of Latitude Press

Whilst the author has walked and researched all the routes for the purposes of this guide, no responsibility can be accepted for any unforeseen circumstances encountered while following them. The publisher would appreciate information regarding material changes.

CONTENTS

INTRODUCTION....................6

THE WALKS (mileage in brackets)
1 East Marton (6^{3}4)................10
2 Crookrise Crag (6^{1}2)............13
3 Embsay Moor (6^{3}4)..............16
4 Ramshaw (6^{3}4)...................20
5 Cononley Lead Mine (6^{3}4)......23
6 Pinhaw Beacon (5^{1}2)...........26
7 Skipton Moor (6)................29
8 Farnhill Moor (6^{1}4).............32
9 Sutton Clough (5)...............35
10 Earl Crag (6^{1}4)..................38
11 Doubler Stones (6^{1}2)...........42
12 Alder Carr Wood (6)............45
13 Newsholme Dean (7)...........48
14 Ponden Clough (5^{3}4)............52
15 Top Withins (6^{1}4)................55
16 Worth Valley (5^{1}4)...............58
17 Brow Moor (5^{3}4).................62
18 Nab Hill (6^{1}2)....................66
19 Black Moor (6^{1}2)................70
20 Harden Moor (5^{1}2)..............74
21 Rombalds Moor (8^{1}2)...........78
22 Riverbank & Towpath (6)......81
23 St Ives & Druid's Altar (6^{1}2)...84
24 Baildon Moor (7^{1}4).............. 88
25 Shipley Glen (6^{1}4)...............92

INDEX.................................96

INTRODUCTION

On leaving the Yorkshire Dales National Park at Gargrave the River Aire begins a fascinating journey through the Pennines. The Aire Valley is populated by towns of substantial size such as Keighley, Bingley and Shipley, yet everywhere it reveals features of immense character and interest. A score of independent villages such as Cononley, Bradley and Cowling are sprinkled at regular intervals along the valley floor, while a little more off the beaten track are gems such as Micklethwaite and Lothersdale.

Between the buzzing market town of Skipton and the World Heritage Site of Saltaire, the Aire winds a largely unfrequented course, paralleled by the more trafficked and colourful Leeds & Liverpool Canal. Hilly flanks rise up on either side towards the popular landmarks of Pinhaw Beacon, Earl Crag, Shipley Glen and the Druid's Altar: lesser known scenic corners include Holden Beck, Sunnydale, Ramshaw and the Doubler Stones. Little valleys are secreted all over the region, some of the finest on offer at Goit Stock, Sutton Clough and Newsholme Dean. Such a well-frequented area has much of man's work on show too, including the Five Rise Locks, Cononley Lead Mine, Hewenden Viaduct and Saltaire.

Though not the area's geographical centre, Haworth makes itself the focal point. It was made internationally famous by the Bronte sisters, who themselves played their part in promoting the surrounding moorland. Haworth looks over the Worth Valley, which aided by its preserved steam railway, drives a wedge into the high moors of the Pennine watershed. Above the neighbouring Bronte Country villages of Oxenhope and Stanbury you find such Worth Valley favourites as Haworth Moor, Ponden Clough and Nab Hill.

Reservoirs and gritstone outcrops occur with regularity hereabouts, while Hirst Wood, Alder Carr Wood and St Ives offer varied woodland walking. Aside from the broad heathery sweeps of the high Pennines, this is also an area of pocket moors, with the likes of Farnhill Moor, Brow Moor, Black Moor and Harden Moor parcelled between villages that are now largely dormitories for neighbouring towns and cities: most are, or until recently were, dominated by 'dark satanic mills', a reminder that this is the colourful fringe of the industrial West Riding. Most of these village centrepieces have been converted to residential use in recent years.

INTRODUCTION

WALKING in YORKSHIRE

AIRE VALLEY
& BRONTE COUNTRY

◆ Walks
● Start points

The area is shared between the Bradford District of West Yorkshire and the Craven District of North Yorkshire: a couple of the walks are within the Yorkshire Dales National Park. A feature of the area is its accessibility from nearby towns and cities, notably the West Yorkshire giants of Bradford and Leeds: proof you needn't travel far to enjoy delightful walking in absorbing surroundings.

INTRODUCTION

The Brontes

Patrick Brunty was born in 1777, eldest of 10 children raised in adversity in County Down. Through a fortunate acquaintance he had the opportunity to study at Cambridge, and amended his name in recognition of his hero Lord Nelson (who had become Duke of Bronte). After a spell in the south of England he came north to Yorkshire, initially to Dewsbury. He began his curacy at Hartshead in 1811, and the following year married Maria Branwell. They took up residence at Hightown where their first two children, Maria and Elizabeth, were born. In 1815 Bronte moved to Thornton, where Charlotte, Patrick Branwell, Emily Jane and Anne were born. No sooner was the family complete then it was on the move to their celebrated home, the parsonage at Haworth. Here all but one were to end their lives, indeed the children lost their mother the very next year. The death of the elder daughters in 1825 left the four other children to attain adulthood.

The three sisters departed on numerous occasions to spend spells as governesses in other parts of the region, while Branwell's promise as an artist soon faltered. After a spell as a railway clerk in the Calder Valley he returned home: stricken by illness he saw out his closing years as a regular of the Black Bull, adjacent to the church. The sisters also returned to the fold to begin their pitifully short literary careers. In an age when such activity by women was frowned upon, their first works appeared under the pseudonyms Currer, Ellis and Acton Bell, with each retaining their initials.

When the first novels were published Emily and Anne had little time to enjoy acclaim, for their deaths rapidly followed the demise of Branwell in 1848. Anne was buried in Scarborough, where the sea air offered no escape from the consumption (tuberculosis) that accounted for all but Charlotte. Charlotte's several novels enjoyed critical acclaim, and she survived long enough to marry her father's curate in 1854. Tragically her flame was also to burn out the very next year, still not 39. Thus Patrick Bronte was to outlive all his children, attaining the ripe old age of 84. What makes the story of the Bronte sisters so memorable is the nature of the background to their literary achievements, notably the adversity the family had faced, and more appreciably still the brooding moorland beyond their Haworth home, where they found untold inspiration: Emily's solitary output *Wuthering Heights* stands as the iconic Bronte work.

INTRODUCTION

Access to the countryside
Walks 2 and 3 make use of the long established Barden Moor access area above Embsay: on most days of the year you are free to walk responsibly over this invigorating landscape. The two most notable restrictions are that dogs are banned from these grouse moors; and that the area can be closed at times of high fire risk, and for up to 28 days each year, subject to advance notice. Most likely times are from the 'Glorious Twelfth', the start of the grouse shooting season in August: Sundays are normally open. Further information can be obtained at *www.boltonabbey.com*.

Using the guide
The walks range from 5 to 8½ miles, with an average distance of 6¼ miles. Each walk is self-contained, with essential information followed by a concise route description and simple map. Dovetailed in between are snippets of information on features along the way: these are placed in *italics* to ensure that the all important route description is easier to locate. Start point postcodes are a rough guide only for those with 'satnav': grid references are more precise!

The sketch maps serve to identify the location of the routes rather than the fine detail, and whilst the description should be sufficient to guide you around, the appropriate Ordnance Survey map is recommended. To gain the most from a walk, the detail of a 1:25,000 scale Explorer map is unsurpassed. It also gives the option to vary walks as desired, giving a much improved picture of your surroundings and the availability of any linking paths for shortening or lengthening walks. Four maps cover all the walks:
- Explorer OL2 - *Yorkshire Dales South/West*
- Explorer OL21 - *South Pennines (covers 16 of the 25 walks)*
- Explorer 288 - *Bradford & Huddersfield*
- Explorer 297 - *Lower Wharfedale & Washburn Valley*

Also very useful for planning are Landranger maps 103 and 104.

Information Centres
Town Hall, High Street **Skipton** BD23 1AH • 01756-792809
2/4 West Lane **Haworth** BD22 8EF • 01535-642329
Salts Mill, Victoria Road **Saltaire** BD18 3LA • 01274-437942
City Hall, Centenary Square **Bradford** BD1 1HY • 01274-433678

WALK 1 EAST MARTON

Easy walking with countless colourful canal attractions

START *Gargrave (SD 931541; BD23 3LX)*

DISTANCE *6¾ miles (10¾km)*

ORDNANCE SURVEY 1:25,000 MAP
Explorer OL2 - Yorkshire Dales South/West

ACCESS *Start from the village centre. Car parks on West Street. Skipton-Settle bus and Leeds-Morecambe/Carlisle trains.*

Gargrave is an attractive village split by the busy A65. Shops and cafes line the main street as it widens into a spacious area where a sturdy bridge crosses the River Aire. Across it is St Andrew's church: restored in 1852, the tower dates from the early 16th century. The Pennine Way passes through the village, and the Old Swan and the Masons Arms provide welcome refreshment. Here also the Leeds-Liverpool Canal reaches the northernmost point of its 127 miles as it meets the National Park boundary.

Cross the bridge over the Aire and turn immediately right on the path upstream. This runs past several houses and alongside a mill-cut, to leave the riverside High Green at a corner and emerge onto a street. Turn left to join Marton Road. Go briefly right, then left on the Scaleber Farm drive. This runs for some time largely between hedgerows and bridging the railway. At this point the Pennine Way joins in, and remains underfoot to East Marton. After

EAST MARTON • WALK 1

climbing to a cattle-grid, turn off the drive at a stile on the left and bear gently away up the field. A track comes up from the right but you soon cross it at right-angles to rise to a stake on the brow. *Lancashire's Pendle Hill dominates the scene ahead, while back over your left shoulder are the heights of Flasby Fell, overtopped by Cracoe Fell with its monument prominent. To the right are the Malhamdale heights of Rye Loaf Hill and Kirkby Fell.*

With Pendle Hill as a guide, advance to a kissing-gate then head away with a fence to a stile at the end. Bear left over the field to the next corner stile, then head away with the fence again. From the next stile drop to a stile by a gate over tiny Crickle Beck. Now bear right, a short way from the fence shadowing the stream, and on through an intervening gate and on again to a fence-end adjacent to a farm bridge by a modern barn. With a sliver of woodland to the right, advance straight on again to a stile, and through several more in succession, closing in on the tree-lined streamlet to drop to a stile in the adjacent hedge. This sees you cross the stream on a plank footbridge. Across, bear left up the field to find a wall-stile in the far bottom corner, joining a rough lane.

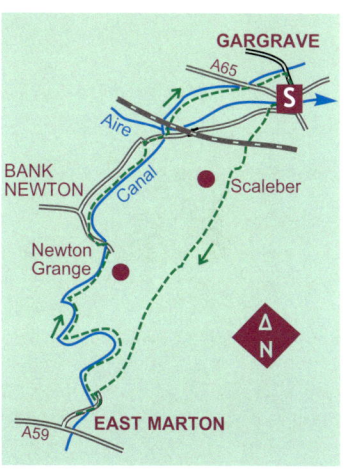

Turn left along the lane and after 200 yards take a stile on the left. *This short section short-cuts a bend in the lane.* Cross the field to a stile on the left of the wood ahead, from where a short-lived walled way rises alongside Langber Plantation. A novel stile at the top sees you back out. Through a small gate a thin path ascends the field, bearing away from the wood to cross to a slim stile at the far corner. This admits onto the now surfaced lane. Follow it left past further recolonised quarries, quickly reaching Williamson Bridge on the canal at East Marton. *There are always plenty of boats moored here, while just ahead, the busy A59 is seen crossing the canal by*

WALK 1 • EAST MARTON

a vertically double-arched bridge. The reason for this strange arrangement is simply the bustling nature of the road: the older, lower arch long superseded by the need for the sturdier, higher one.

Your return route takes to the towpath here, but the hamlet itself may first merit some attention. Continuing straight over the bridge, some attractive housing is passed - that to the right sports mullioned windows, while alongside is a tearoom. Just up the lane, alongside the A59, is the Cross Keys pub and a small green, while St Peter's church is hidden on the other side of the main road. Back at the canal, double back under Williamson Bridge to begin the return. Here the route description effectively comes to an end, for though the walk is not yet halfway through, all that remains is to follow the waterway back to Gargrave. Its various meanderings ensure this is a longer return, especially in the early stages. *A glance at the OS map confirms the canal's dogged attempts to maintain its contour result in an appreciable weaving journey. This section has a curiously remote feeling to it. Increasingly, Flasby Fell forms a colourful backdrop, flanked by Cracoe Fell and Embsay Crag.*

Approaching Bank Newton an old milestone features the waterway's extremities of Liverpool and Leeds. The old lane is then briefly rejoined before it crosses the canal. Double back under the road bridge to regain the towpath just short of the first of Bank Newton's locks. There now follows a splendid string of such locks, seven in all. *This section is full of interest, and summer weekends see much activity by the boating fraternity. An old lock-keeper's house at Legaston Bank bears a 1791 datestone.*

The moorings follow the locks, beyond which another short road section is forced until reaching the next bridge. Doubling back underneath Priest Holme Bridge, the bank offers immediate further interest, first in an aqueduct above the River Aire, then straight under the railway, with its viaduct over the river just downstream. The final section sees Gargrave's scattered locks begin, the third being alongside the Anchor Inn. The canal then takes you under the main road to conclude around the back of the village. At the road bridge at Higherland Lock, finally abandon the towpath and turn right down the road to re-enter the village alongside the main car park.

CROOKRISE CRAG

WALK 2

Entirely moorland walking visiting Barden Moor landmarks

START Embsay (SD 998544; BD23 6PP)

DISTANCE $6^{1}/_{2}$ miles ($10^{1}/_{2}$km)

ORDNANCE SURVEY 1:25,000 MAP
Explorer OL2 - Yorkshire Dales South/West

ACCESS Start from Embsay Reservoir, reached by Pasture Road off Elm Tree Square at top of village. Water company car park.
• OPEN ACCESS: see page 9.

Embsay Reservoir enjoys a fine setting under Embsay Crag and Moor, its facilities shared by sailing and angling clubs: the short reservoir circuit is a popular stroll. From the car park head left on the enclosed track outside the reservoir wall, past the sailing club to the far end. Through a gate leave the access road as it swings left towards a lone house at Crag Nook, and instead take a stile in the fence to gain the foot of the open moor at an information board. Turn left onto a path beginning an immediate climb through a few reeds and quickly improving in bracken. Shortly it swings left to rise towards the wall there. The path climbs close by the wall, rising through a few scattered boulders then into a bouldery gully. Now hard by the wall, it emerges onto the open heather moor. Soon the first of several stiles in the wall is reached: use it to attain the top of the cliffs of Crookrise Crag, a breathtaking moment.

WALK 2 • CROOKRISE CRAG

The panorama stretches from the Aire Valley and South Pennines round to Pendle Hill, Longridge Fell and Bowland; Ingleborough peeks over Rye Loaf Hill and Kirkby Fell. Flasby Fell's little peaks are just in front, while the higher reaches of the Dales fill the rest of the scene to the north. Now confined in the narrow space between the steep drop and the wall, continue northward on a thin path straight towards the OS column which soon appears ahead. *At 1361ft/415m, this is Crookrise Crag Top. The expanse of heather-clad upland known as Barden Moor comes to an abrupt halt at many places around its rim, but nowhere as dramatically as Crookrise, where a long line of crags fall steeply to a carpet of conifers. The crags are substantial enough to offer a varied range of challenges for rock climbers. Additions to the panorama are neighbouring Rylstone Fell and Cracoe Fell to the north, with Buckden Pike far beyond.*

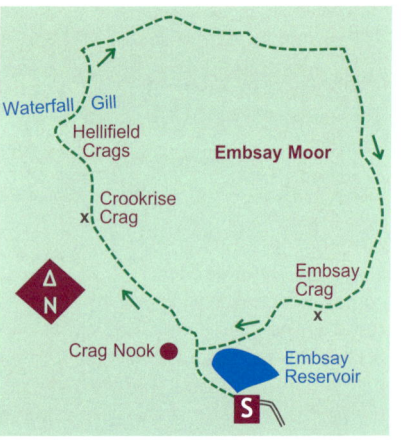

A stile returns you to the moorland side of the wall to continue north over small boulders. Path and wall remain close as denser bracken takes over, dropping to pass beneath the enormous blocky boulders of Fairies Chest. After a moist level section the wall drops away, taking the trees with it: the clear path maintains a level course to quickly arrive above a steep plunge to Waterfall Gill, a splendid moment. The drop is largely avoided as the path slants right beneath the extensive boulders of Hellifield Crags. Just before reaching the beck a fine waterfall is seen from above. Across, the path climbs steeply through bracken to meet a sturdy wall. The gradient eases and the nearby wall shadows a gentle rise to a gate where the Rylstone-Bolton Abbey bridleway passes through.

Turn right along it, remaining underfoot for almost a mile and a half. *This historic route was immortalised by Wordsworth in his*

CROOKRISE CRAG • WALK 2

poem 'The White Doe of Rylstone'. The story of the ill-fated Nortons of Rylstone tells of a widow undertaking the trek over the moor to visit her husband's grave at Bolton Priory: the pet deer that accompanied her continued the journeys even after her death. Followed onto the heart of the moor, this near-level path has been largely restored with a more durable surface. As a more regular path it crosses a marshy streamlet, soon returning to its stronger base for a steady rise to quickly merge into a traditional shooters' track coming up from a pair of thatched cabins. Continue to stride out in grand style, rising ever gradually to the brow of the hill.

The walk's summit at 1410ft/430m sees scattered rocks to your left and Simon's Seat on the skyline far ahead. Leave the track on a thin path to the right, crossing a gentle dip before a level stroll. *As the ground opens up, sweeping views look south to Rombalds Moor and the South Pennines.* Whilst still level, ignore a thinner branch rising slightly left. Further, a cairn marks the start of a sustained, gentle descent through heather as Embsay Crag appears ahead. After a brief moist spell the path runs through a final heather groove to emerge above reedy slopes: Embsay Crag has grown in stature. Continue down, slanting right until the path is about to commence a steeper, grooved descent towards the intake wall just below. Instead branch right to a few boulders on a knoll just across a few reeds. As Embsay Crag returns ahead, a sheeptrod contours above a steeper drop left, with a heathery brow on your right. This leads easily along to a saddle at the rear of Embsay Crag. A thin path comes in from the right and rises more broadly up through heather towards the crest, merging into a broader path for the final few feet, with a steep, bouldery hollow on your left.

Jutting out from the moor, 1217ft/371m Embsay Crag is a notable landmark in the Skipton area. The highest rocks are the perfect location for a long, lazy break on a summer's day, with the reservoir shimmering far below. While a direct path descends the steepest section just below, a friendlier start is to follow a clear path along the brink of the rocks slanting down to the right. After exchanging heather for dense bracken it drops a little more steeply to swing left to meet the main path down from the crag. This leads unerringly down to a footbridge outside the reservoir head. Across it ascend briefly, and the path bears right to join a broader green one which runs left to the stile back off the moor.

WALK 3
EMBSAY MOOR

Big moorland strides with vistas to match

START *Embsay (SE 009538; BD23 6RB)*

DISTANCE $6\frac{3}{4}$ *miles ($10\frac{3}{4}$km)*

ORDNANCE SURVEY 1:25,000 MAP
Explorer OL2 - Yorkshire Dales South/West

ACCESS *Start from Elm Tree Square at top of village. Car park along street. Bus from Skipton. • OPEN ACCESS: see page 9.*

Partly inside the Yorkshire Dales National Park boundary, Embsay is a thriving village sandwiched between Skipton and the moors. It is home to the preserved Embsay & Bolton Abbey Steam Railway, painstakingly restored to Bolton Abbey station, a return trip of some 12 miles on the old Skipton-Ilkley line: it has giftshop and refreshments. There are two pubs, the Cavendish and the Elm Tree, and a Post office/shop. Leave by a kissing-gate at the back of the car park, and bear left to a stile at the top corner of the field. *Up to the right are the bracken flanks of Embsay Crag, with Crookrise Crag set back to its left: both are visited on WALK 2.*

The slender path slants up to a bridle-gate, then crosses the fields behind the school and houses. Over a pair of stiles at a farm track at the end, bear left to the next stile and then right to the next. Advance on through another and on through a redundant gateway. Approaching Manor House Farm on the right, advance on

EMBSAY MOOR • WALK 3

to drop to a corner stile onto Pasture Road opposite a millpond. *This is popular with ducks, while the distinguished Manor House overlooking it just to the left bears a 1665 datestone.*

Turn right on the lane rising to the grassy dam of Embsay Reservoir. *The old chimney from Spindle Mill is just across to the right, while Pendle Hill is an early part of the view to the south-west. Ahead, Embsay Crag is over to the right, with the beginnings of Crookrise Crag to the left, but of more relevance is the rocky outcrop of Deer Gallows just breaking the skyline ahead.* Bear left to the reservoir corner and advance along the enclosed

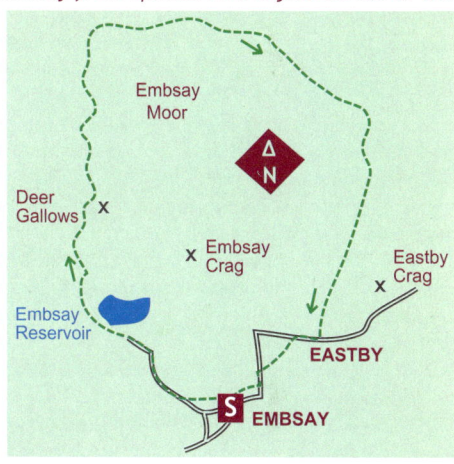

stony access road alongside. *A parallel alternative path takes a bridle-gate after the sailing club to run a grassy course between wall and reservoir, keeping left at a fork at the water's end to run on to a gate back onto the access road.* Through a gateway leave the access road as it swings left towards a lone house at Crag Nook, and instead take a stile in the fence on your right to gain the foot of the open moor at an information board.

A level green path heads away above the wall. Within 100 yards, after crossing a pair of marshy streamlets, turn left at the end of the bracken to ascend the pleasant, largely pathless moor-grass slope. Not far directly above is your objective of a slanting, grooved way. Through a small tract of bracken you encounter a good path, slanting steeply right to merge with the aforementioned distinct grooved way. Follow this up to a sharp bend left, and remain with it to quickly fade and ascend more directly on easier slopes: Deer Gallows appears again over to the right and not a great deal higher.

WALK 3 • EMBSAY MOOR

The surroundings are magnificent, with Embsay Crag across to the right and a bird's-eye view of the reservoir. Look back over Skipton to the Aire Valley backed by the high Pennine watershed, re-forming after the major interruption of the Aire Gap. Now no more than a thin trod angling slightly right, it is better to continue straight up pleasant moor-grass to avoid a damp, heathery section. Rise to the left of a small cluster of boulders at Mossley Stones, atop which angle further right on increasingly gentler ground to merge through reeds into a distinct path.

The gritstone rocks of Deer Gallows are by now marginally set back below you beyond a line of grouse butts. The detour to these outcrops is a mere five-minute level march on a thin but clear path curving off the main path, possibly just a little back (depending on where you joined the main path), close by a small pile of stones. It passes near a shooting butt en route to the rocks. *This superb spot is popular with climbers, with the main cliff face of millstone grit tilted gently back and riven by some great rounded gashes. Facing it just across a green floor is the added attraction of a rock tower, composed of exactly the same layout, block upon block.*

Return to the path and resume, now almost level, with a marshy tract on your left. The firm grassy path forges on the final stages to the brow, a very gentle and pleasant rise across the increasingly heathery moor, with a line of butts over to the right. It gradually transforms into a firmer track just short of the brow of East Harts Hill. *This brings a magnificent prospect of the interior of the moor. Cracoe Fell's obelisk sits on the skyline ahead. In late summer these rolling heather seas are positively outstanding. Look back to a sweeping panorama of the South Pennines, Pendle Hill, Longridge Fell and the Bowland moors, the Malhamdale hills of Rye Loaf Hill and Kirkby Fell, mighty Ingleborough and Fountains Fell.*

Simply remain on this excellent track to commence a long, steady descent to the beginnings of Waterfall Gill and rising to a pair of shooters' cabins. *These come as a surprise, traditionally constructed of local stone with a bilberry thatch-like topping!* Curving up to the right your track absorbs a bridleway coming in from the left. *This historic route was immortalised by Wordsworth in his poem 'The White Doe of Rylstone'. The story of the ill-fated Nortons of Rylstone tells of a widow undertaking the trek over the moor to visit her husband's grave at Bolton Priory: the pet deer*

EMBSAY MOOR • WALK 3

that accompanied her continued the journeys even after her death. Remain on the shooters' track which runs eastwards, encouraging long strides on a grand, gently rising course.

Scattered rocks are met on the track summit at 1410ft/430m, just beyond which, ignore a track heading off left to Upper Barden Reservoir, which appears at this point. *A new view is revealed ahead as Simon's Seat appears across delectable Wharfedale, and soon Lower Barden Reservoir comes into the scene below.* The excellent track spends some time running a near-level, extended promenade before descending more markedly, curving down to the right to level out at a sharp bend. At the fork here opt for the inviting track rising right into a minor hollow, passing beneath a stone shooters' cabin. Just beyond is an inferior cabin, but your track turns up to the right just before it. Keep left as an early lesser one bears right, to curve up (becoming grassy) to the start of a row of butts. Ignore another right fork here and simply follow the path shadowing the butts, gradually losing both height and heather en route to the last one. *Embsay Crag is well seen over to the right, while ahead Skipton Moor rises above a big quarry, with the Rombalds Moor skyline back to its left.*

At the final butt a thin trod bears gently left down to a ladder-stile off the moor at Eastby Gate. Pass through some sheep pens and turn right down the grassy wallside track through a couple of ladder-stiles to the edge of Heugh Gill. *A nice moment is gained above this side gill, with Embsay Crag's profile now acquiring an exalted status.* The continuing grassy path descends above the gill to a stile onto a track, crossing straight over and soon narrowing to become deeply ensconced in a hollowed, leafy way. Over a stile at the bottom you emerge into a yard at Hunters Croft and down onto the road through Eastby. *This tiny farming village is strung along the road over the moor to Barden, and until 2009 it had a pub, the Masons Arms.*

Turn right, leaving the village and then leaving the road at a path on the left. There is a certain quaintness to the tarmac strip of path, not more than a foot wide as it runs through the fields to Embsay's church of St Mary the Virgin. At the road, follow it left a little past the church, then take a stile on the right. Head across to a corner stile, from where an enclosed path runs to emerge via a final stile into the field above the car park.

WALK 4 RAMSHAW

Wooded becks, open country, big views and a riverbank

START *Carleton (SD 972496; BD23 3DR)*

DISTANCE *6¾ miles (10¾km)*

ORDNANCE SURVEY 1:25,000 MAP
Explorer OL21 - South Pennines

ACCESS *Start from the village centre. Roadside parking. Bus from Skipton.*

Carleton-in-Craven (Sunday name) looks across the Aire Gap to the Yorkshire Dales. Grouped around its large 140-year old mill (now residential) are the Swan pub (and cafe), Post office, shop and St Mary's church. Head west on the Colne road, and at the end of the mill turn left along an enclosed snicket immediately before Catlow Gill. This rises away by the beck, and before reaching a flight of steps, take a right fork to remain above the beck. This curves around through trees to meet an access road at a bridge. Go left on this to run parallel with the beck. Beyond farm buildings it emerges to a gate into a field.

The grassy path runs through several fields with the tree-lined beck down to the right. At a pronounced bend in the beck, turn upstream on the rim of the steep-sided gill. Part way up the field it is apparent you're now above a side beck, and a marker post sends a faint path slanting into the floor of the gill. Cross a stile and the stream, and a path winds up the opposite bank. Resume left atop the bank up to a wall-stile ahead. *Look back to see the expanse of Barden Moor behind Skipton.* Slant right up a large field to a gate at the top right, on the rim of Carleton Glen. Contour across and then down to the beck in a gap in the trees. Across, go a few yards up to a stile in a short length of wall. Climb away again and resume left above the bank, again to a wall-stile. Now ascend the field to Gawthorpe House, joining its drive at a stile in front. Turn left and leave the drive on a short grassy track descending to a gate. Across a tiny stream, advance on this grassy little pasture to a gate at the end.

Entering a pocket moorland pasture, the path bears right up the wallside to find a bridle-gate onto Park Lane. Head up this the short way to a T-junction and turn left, quickly leaving the adjacent plantation

behind. Passing a lesser right fork, the road drops gently to arrive at Tewit Cote farm road on a bend. *Nice views look over Lothers Dale and across to Earl Crag.* Go left on this, and as it drops towards the house hidden in trees, instead contour left along a grassy track to a wall-stile in the far corner, just up from a gate.

Entering the rough moorland of Burnt Hill, a thin path follows the wall to a kink, where a gateway takes the path to the other side. After a reedy corner, a good track follows the wall the short way down to a slight dip with a wall junction on the left. Here the track heads off right, but your way is through the adjacent gate. Ignore the track dropping away with the wall, and resume on a pleasant little path again along the west side of the level moorland ridge of Ramshaw. This narrows before reaching the abrupt start of

WALK 4 • RAMSHAW

the descent. *Despite the planting of random, alien conifers this heathery crest is a delight, views over countless Airedale villages and landmarks extending to an array of Dales fells.*

Drop off the steep end with the wall, through a corner stile off the moor and down a fieldside. Through a small gate at the bottom by-pass Carleton Biggin via adjacent gates to a stile in a wall-kink. A little enclosed path swings right to emerge onto its drive outside the gate. Turn left down the drive, and with a road in sight, stiles are reached on both sides. From the right-hand stile head across the field, over a slight brow and on to the far end, where a corner stile puts you onto a road. Go right a few strides and escape at a wall-stile on the left. Bear right across the top of this sloping field, slanting gently down around a hollow to a gate opposite. Now head away with a crumbling wall down to a gate at Throstle Nest Farm.

Through the gate advance on past the house and down the field, merging with the fence on your right. Towards the corner take a stile in it and go left on an enclosed green way curving round to end at a gate outside another house at Cononley Woodside. Again advance on past the house, but at the end of its grounds as its drive begins, turn sharp left immediately after crossing a tiny stream. Follow it left to a small footbridge on a sidestream, then head away alongside the hedge on the left into a corner in front of the railway line. Over a footbridge on the stream, a wall-stile accesses the busy line. Over the crossing to another stile, head away with a fence on your right. At the end a stile conveys you to the other side alongside a drain, resuming alongside a fence to quickly arrive at the flood embankment hiding the River Aire.

Now simply turn left on the bank, encountering several gates/stiles as its winds lazily around. Reaching a wall-stile beneath a rail bridge, pass beneath and resume as before. At a bend right just ahead, the right of way officially bears left across the field onto Pale Lane, but common practice remains true to the bank to wind around to a gate/stile at Carleton Bridge. Go right the few strides to a junction, then left on the footway along the Carleton road. Absorbing Carla Beck Lane at the village edge, the footway transfers to the other side to re-enter the village. *On your left is Spence's Court, 17th century almshouses with spinning galleries above a courtyard.* The finish can be varied by squeezing between houses on the right, where a flagged path runs on to the church.

CONONLEY LEAD MINE

WALK 5

Easy walking, absorbing industrial archaeology, super views

START Cononley (SD 989469; BD20 8NR)

DISTANCE 6¾ miles (10¾km)

ORDNANCE SURVEY 1:25,000 MAP
Explorer OL21 - South Pennines

ACCESS Start from the village centre. Small car park where Meadow Lane meets Main Street, also roadside parking. Keighley-Skipton bus and train.

Cononley is a traditional Airedale village whose former mill is finally seeing conversion to residential use. In among attractive old cottages are two pubs, the New Inn and the Railway. From the bridge by the Post office/shop walk up Main Street past the New Inn, and leave by an access road on the left after Cononley Hall and along the near side of the Institute. It bridges the beck and climbs steeply away, becoming enclosed part way up. As it turns right for Town Head Farm at a sharp bend, continue straight up a walled green way. Through a gate at the top turn right to accompany a gradually rising wall on an improving grassy track. *Look back for good views over the village and up the Aire Valley into the Dales.*

Beyond a stile at a blocked gate it improves further, easing out to reach the houses at Great Gib and Little Gib. *At this very early stage in the walk, virtually all its climbing is over!* Stiles lead past

WALK 5 • CONONLEY LEAD MINE

the rear of the houses, then advance straight on their access road, which quickly swings right to pass Cononley Lead Mine. *A little gate gives access to the restored workings dominated by a chimney and Cornish-style engine house. These imposing remains of Yorkshire's southernmost lead mine stand isolated from the extensive workings at Grassington Moor above Wharfedale. Long part of the Duke of Devonshire's vast lands, the buildings date from around 1842, as does the reservoir across the access road. Mining ceased in 1882.*

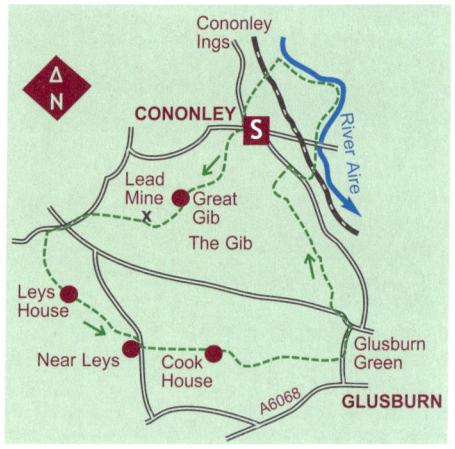

The access road leads out onto a road, where go left to a lone house at Four Lane Ends. Cross straight over on the Lothersdale road, and opposite the buildings on your right, drop left to a stile by a gate. A track drops down into the field below, escaping detritus before joining the wall on your left. From a corner stile above a wood, cross to another just a few yards beyond it, and now traverse two field tops to Leys House. *This stage enjoys views south to Earl Crag and its two monuments.* The garden is entered by a stile just down the wall, emerging between the houses onto an access road. As this climbs away, from the stile in front resume as before, across a couple of steep field tops towards Near Leys Farm ahead. Advance to the gate just above it, beneath which is a wall-stile onto Leys Lane.

Drop down just past the farm to a stile on the left. Head off along the wallside through several fields. Entering the field just in front of the first building, Cook House, the locally used option keeps straight on along the rear of the house, then dropping right through a gateway to meet the true right of way at a gate/stile just below/left. The less obvious right of way immediately takes a poor

CONONLEY LEAD MINE • WALK 5

stile on the right, passes right of the buildings to a stile in front of the house, out through a gate and straight on to a gate/stile just in front - meeting the unofficial way. Cross the field top to a stile just short of the corner, and then slant down the next field to the houses at West Closes. Turn left along the access road, which leads past several farms to ultimately join Green Lane at Glusburn Green.

Go left past some desirable residences to the Lothersdale road and turn left for a few minutes. Just before Well Spring Farm, a stile/gate on the right send a grassy wallside track away. A kissing-gate at the end sends you past an old concrete reservoir to emerge into the open on a super green way. *Extensive views see the Aire Valley stretch for miles in both directions. Across it are Rombalds, Farnhill and Skipton Moors, while behind Skipton are the shapely tops of Flasby Fell, as well as Barden Moor. Villages on show include Cononley, Bradley, Farnhill and Cross Hills.* The path runs on through an old stile and slants down to a gate to meet a grassy track on a hairpin bend. This drops slightly across a large bracken pasture to a gate in a wall at the end. Cross over a farm track above Gibside and continue along the wallside, reaching a stile just short of the end. Descend the paddock and down through a couple of gates onto an access road, which drops down as Windle Lane onto the road on the village edge. *For a direct finish go left back into the centre.*

The full route turns right out of the village and down to houses on a bend. From a ladder-stile on the left cross the busy railway line, and a nice embanked path heads upstream with the River Aire. Through a kissing-gate at the end it runs a firm, enclosed course along to a gap-stile on the right onto the road alongside Cononley Bridge. Cross over the road to another stile and resume upstream, with a choice of embankment or riverbank. This lovely stroll runs for a long half-mile around the flats of Cononley Ings, passing through an early stile and then a couple of kissing-gates during a sweeping curve back left. Reaching a kissing-gate with another just a few strides further at an outflow, this is the point to leave the river. Rise left over the embankment and down to a gap-stile below. Just yards to the right join the stony track of Shady Lane, and follow its hedgerowed course left, all the way back into the village. The railway is re-crossed, and at the end you emerge back into the village. *Note the old street sign on a house wall, the former Crown Inn.* Turn left along the street back into the centre.

WALK 6
PINHAW BEACON

Enjoyable ups and downs lead to a moorland landmark

START *Lothersdale (SD 959459; BD20 8EL)*

DISTANCE *5½ miles (8¾km)*

ORDNANCE SURVEY 1:25,000 MAP
Explorer OL21 - South Pennines

ACCESS *Start from the village centre. Roadside parking.*

Lothersdale is a highly attractive village strung along a quiet back road, very much off the beaten track. Its seclusion among folds of the hills did not prevent the arrival of the mill age, and the surviving chimney is often all that can be seen of the village. Christ Church stands high and isolated, while a nearby limestone quarry has unearthed prehistoric bones. From the Hare & Hounds pub take an access road almost opposite into a former mill yard. Head on through, with the mill to the right and houses to the left. Just before the end turn right on a short-lived access road between further houses and mill, and over a small footbridge at the end.

From a stile beneath the chimney, a path heads downstream with Leys Beck on your left, through a kissing-gate into pleasant surroundings. Ignoring a footbridge by a concrete ford, advance to the end where a footbridge on a streamlet accesses a corner stile as the beck swings away to the left. *An easy mistake is to continue unimpeded downstream to the next footbridge on the beck.*

PINHAW BEACON • WALK 6

Properly, the invisible path rises right up the bank, meeting a wall to lead on to a corner stile by an old gate. A lovely enclosed path heads away, but is left within a few paces at a wall-stile on the left. From one just behind it descend the field, bearing right to pass through a wall-stile and down to another stile just below. Now drop down the minor bank and cross to a footbridge on the beck.

Across, clamber up the initial bank then rise right up the large sloping field: up to your left is the impressive Stone Gappe. *Here, briefly, Charlotte Bronte was governess, and it became the Gateshead Hall of 'Jane Eyre'.* Joining a tree-lined stream, ascend outside the clough, becoming enclosed by a wall to reach a gateway at the top. Now bear right again to resume with another rising wall, meeting a track from the left to skirt detritus to a gate/stile, just above which it joins a road. Turn right to a crossroads. *This spell enjoys big views east beyond Cononley Lead Mine and the Gib.* Turn left on Babyhouse Lane, the road climbing before it eases out. At a distinct bend right, leave by a stile alongside a gate on the left. *The gatepost here is in fact a recycled guidepost with names of towns inscribed.*

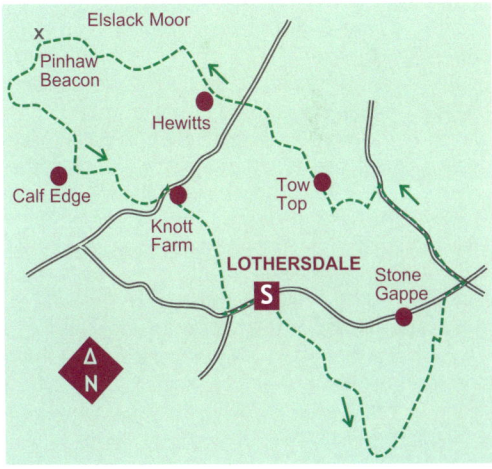

Cross the field corner to an outer wall corner just ahead, then a part embanked way follows the right-hand wall rising gently along the field top. A stile at the end puts you onto an access road, Tow Top Lane. Turn left down this, quickly swinging right to drop to Tow Top Farm. Don't enter but keep left on a continuing grassy way between walls. It drops to bridge a streamlet then rises away to a gate/stile, from where a path runs

WALK 6 • PINHAW BEACON

by the continuing right-hand wall. When it bends right at a tiny stream the path does likewise, rising to a gate/stile at the end where the route of the Pennine Way is joined. Pass through and rise to a gate/stile at the top onto a road.

Cross straight over and up Hewitts farm road. When it goes left pass through a gate/stile to keep straight on up an enclosed grassy way broadening into a field, then up the wallside on your left to a stile onto Elslack Moor. A path ascends the wallside on your left, then runs left with it on a flagged section before breaking free at another wall corner to rise gradually to Pinhaw. Within 300 yards of the top a grass path doubles back right to Robert Wilson's Grave. *Its fading course runs 130 yards down the slope to an inscribed stone. Robert Wilson perished here in 1805, one of the guards who manned Pinhaw Beacon: three surrounding parishes shared the duties.* The broad path runs on to the OS column at 1273ft/388m on Pinhaw. *The summit is discernible as the raised site of the aforementioned beacon, one of a chain that stretched across the country to warn of impending danger or to celebrate major events. Finest feature in this extensive panorama are the Yorkshire Dales fells.*

Two paths leave, but merge within 100 paces amid heathery knolls. A wall corner is quickly reached, and here the PW is finally left. Take a contrastingly thin path running left with the wall, and beyond a small marsh, over a tiny brow. The path curves left above a wall corner and along to a stile off the moor. Amid a few newly planted trees bear left to a fence-stile below, then left a few strides above a wood corner to a gate/stile into a sizeable field. Slant diagonally down this to a gate/stile near the bottom corner, and descend the wallside to a stile onto a drive at Calf Edge Farm.

Go left on this drive which runs on to a junction, where keep right to drop down onto a back road. Go left for two minutes, and over a stream turn right down a short driveway to Knott Farm. *This splendid house boasts mullioned windows and a 1695 datestone.* Go straight on down a short track curving left to the front of the house, then from the left-hand gate a grassy track runs on with a wall on your left. At the end of a second field it swings right to a corner gateway. Head straight down the wallside, with the village millpond below. At the bottom corner ignore the gate in favour of a wall-stile in front. Drop down to another stile, and a small bridge over the outflow onto the road in the village. Go left to finish.

SKIPTON MOOR

WALK 7

Richly varied walking from an attractive village, featuring fieldpaths, moorland and canal towpath

START *Bradley (SE 000482; BD20 9EL)*

DISTANCE *6 miles (9½km)*

ORDNANCE SURVEY 1:25,000 MAP
Explorer OL21 - South Pennines

ACCESS *Start from canal swing-bridge on road into village, car park alongside. Skipton-Keighley bus on main road.*

From the canal bridge head up Ings Lane past sports fields into the village, and at a T-junction by the shop take a snicket opposite alongside the Methodist church of 1897. *Though the nucleus of the village is actually Low Bradley in deference to the farming hamlet of High Bradley high on the flanks of the Standard, in practice the whole place is simply Bradley.* Emerging onto a lane through a small modern development, turn left to the imposing Old Hall at the end. *Bearing a 1678 datestone, it forms a magnificent front to a working farm. Just back along the road to the right is the less obvious yet similarly impressive College House. Bradley's pub is the cozy Slaters Arms.*

Left of the hall a snicket emerges into a field: head away along the wallside to a stile at the end. Ahead is the fine three-storey Ghyll Farm. Slant right to a small gate in the hedge above,

WALK 7 • SKIPTON MOOR

descending steps to the edge of the garden. Without entering take a small gate on the right to ascend a large field, close by the wall on the left. This tapers to a gate at the top, with a green lane on your right. Bear left to ascend by deep-cut North Beck, over an intervening wall-stile to a gate at the top. *With gorse in flower the hollow on your left is a riot of colour.* Go left onto a firmer track, rising to absorb Lower House Farm drive beneath the farm, then up to Higher House. Just beyond, in an unkempt little enclosure, use a wall-stile at the top (between corner gates) to bear left on a wallside track, crossing to a stile between adjacent gates ahead.

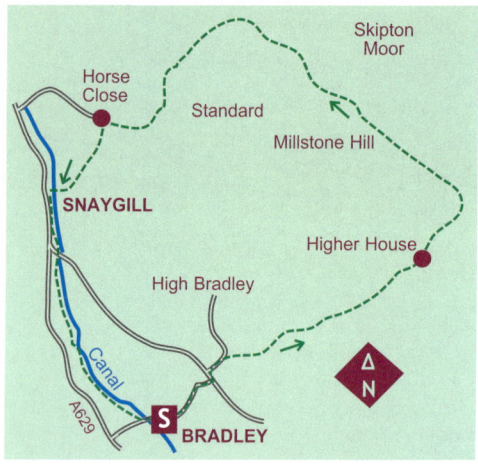

Head up the fieldside to a small barn, then bear left up to the top corner: the left-hand of two stiles admits to a tract of rough pasture. *By now you savour massive views over the Aire Valley to the long skyline of the South Pennines, featuring Boulsworth Hill and Pinhaw.* Slant up once more on a thin path to a tumbledown stile in a kink in the top wall to enter an area of reedy moor-grass. A thin path maintains the line up a tussocky pasture to boulders on Millstone Hill. This reveals the bog of Black Sike, and the highest point of the Standard across to the left, with the stony edge of Standard Crag beyond the marsh. Strike a bee-line for a distant wall-corner left of the marsh, evading its excesses by crossing at the outflow.

SKIPTON MOOR • WALK 7

When a wall comes up from the left, easier going on a broader path brings arrival at a stile in the corner, on the Standard. *This is a stunning moment, with a fine prospect of the Aire Gap beyond the moor, and a bird's-eye view of Skipton: beyond are the hills of Craven. Prominent across to the right and marked by several stone men is the summit of Skipton Moor at 1224ft/373m.*

A sunken way winds down in the Skipton direction, bearing right in a graceful curve away from the wall on your left. Beyond the head of a marshy area another path is met and you drop left to a stile above a gate in the wall corner. A broad path drops away, again a little to the right. Lower, it bends right alongside a minor knoll with scattered rocks: approaching gorse patches, here take a less obvious left fork which appears to drop into marshy surrounds. These prove negligible, and the initially faint path improves to drop further left, converging with the wall down to a good stile built into it just short of the tapering bottom wall corner.

From the stile, angle gently right away from the wall, dropping slightly and passing above some boulders on a largely level course. A grassy track slowly forms to drop to a gate in the wall below. From the adjacent stile slant left down the field to find a wall-stile just above a gate in the bottom corner. Entering the moist, wooded environs of Cawder Gill turn down the wallside, a track forming to drop to a gate/stile out into a field. Beyond a wall-corner advance to a track just short of Cawder Hall. Go left down this to a stile by a gate to join the main drive to the hall. Just beyond it, level with the first building at Horse Close Farm, pass through a small gate on the left to double back a few strides to a stile in the wall corner. Ahead is civilisation in the form of a large modern hotel, industrial estate and main road at Snaygill.

Head across the field, dropping gently right and around the base of a knoll to find a wall-stile. A little path then shadows a hummocky crest to meet a rough track dropping gently to a gate in the bottom corner onto an access road. Go left the few strides onto a lane at Snaygill swing-bridge (Low Snaygill). Cross the canal and turn left on the towpath for a long, final mile. The Bay Horse pub is passed before reaching Snaygill Bridge and its colourful boats. The noise of the parallel road is escaped by swinging back towards Bradley, a pleasant return to the village. *Towards the end a canal milestone advises the distances to Leeds and Liverpool.*

WALK 8
FARNHILL MOOR

A delectable pocket moorland and a fine stretch of canal

START *Kildwick (SE 010458; BD20 9BH)*

DISTANCE *6¼ miles (10km)*

ORDNANCE SURVEY 1:25,000 MAP
Explorer OL21 - South Pennines

ACCESS *Start from the corner by pub and church. Parking on old road opposite. Keighley-Skipton bus.*

Kildwick sits back from the bustle of the Aire Valley, though it still catches the sight and sound of traffic bearing down on its roundabout. Church, White Lion Inn, cottages and bridge combine to create a delightful picture: the bridge is one of the oldest on the Aire, rebuilt by the canons of Bolton Priory in 1305 though since widened. Take the road up the left side of the church, going right past the old schoolhouse. *St Andrew's church - the 'Lang Kirk o'Craven' - is a beautiful old building, with an imposing tower and a low-slung roof. Within is a good deal of carved oak, and the remains of 10th century Anglo-Saxon crosses - two of which bear figures. Note also the de Styveton monument of 1307.*

Cross the arched Parson's Bridge on the Leeds-Liverpool Canal, and a flagged snicket rises to a stile into a slim pasture, rising, still flagged, to a higher one onto a driveway, with a road just above. Just to the right is Kildwick Hall. *This splendid 17th century manor*

FARNHILL MOOR • WALK 8

house displays a gabled front, with mullioned and transomed windows. Lions guard the gates, with a coat of arms above the door.
The route goes left, soon leaving the road opposite Starkey Lane by a briefly enclosed path on the right. Through a kissing-gate it rises onto the edge of Farnhill Moor, whose heathery surrounds open pleasantly out. The main path heads directly away, rising gently and running to the farm at Crag Top. Through a gate to its left the main body of the moor is underfoot. At a near immediate fork remain on the main path to the left, rising above old quarries and then more thinly but always clearly through bracken, scrub and scattered trees before rising again to the Jubilee Tower.

Locally 'Farnhill Pinnacle', this 12ft monument was erected in 1887 to commemorate Queen Victoria's Golden Jubilee. Words carved on an adjacent stone record its restoration in 1935 on the occasion of the Silver Jubilee of King George V. Alongside is a seat from which to survey the outstanding Aire Valley vista. Across the valley is Cononley, while meandering below is a good length of the canal: down-dale Earl Crag and its monuments patrol the skyline, while behind Skipton town the peaks of Flasby Fell are prominent.

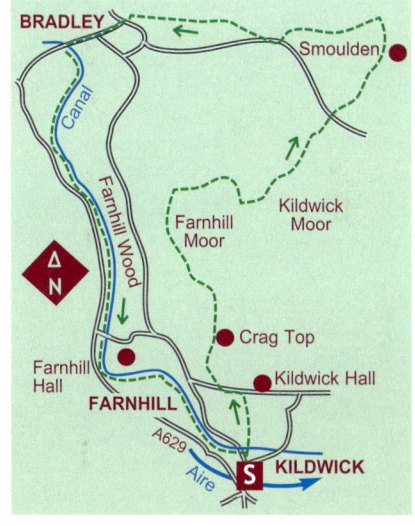

Leave by returning to the path crossroads a few yards east of the pinnacle, and turn left on a clear path maintaining your earlier direction. Rising slightly through bracken and scattered silver birch into heather, it bears right to quickly meet a sturdy wall. Turn right on the parallel path, dropping gently towards Tewit Mire and evading it by swinging right. Quickly forking, keep right to run past more silver birch to soon reach a crossroads with a direct path from the

WALK 8 • FARNHILL MOOR

pinnacle. Turn left here, through a small moist section before opening out again to soon reach a wall-stile off the moor.

Entering the largely grassy Kildwick Moor, the path turns left through a pocket of bracken, then across the centre of this level pasture, bearing right to a corner wall-stile. Entering a field, a faint path bears gently left to a stile in the facing wall. A thin path bears gently right across a larger pasture, rising slightly to an outer wall corner to resume alongside the wall to a stile by a gate onto Jackson's Lane. Cross to a cattle-grid and head directly away on a wallside farm road. After a gate it bears right to Smoulden, but you instead bear left across the field to a corner stile/gate. Cross to a wall-stile opposite, then bear left to one in the facing wall. Now head away left with the wall, through a gate/stile and then slowly curving down to the right with it. Before the bottom take a gate in it, and slant right down to the bottom wall. A grassy track runs left the short way to a stile/gate back out onto Jackson's Lane.

Turn right for a couple of minutes and leave by a wall-stile by a gate on the right. Ignore the track heading away and turn left, close by the wall to drop down to a neat wall-stile in the bottom corner recess just left of two gates. Through this simply descend a series of fields with the wall on your right, each linked by sturdy stiles. At the bottom drop briefly down to a wall-stile onto a grassy walled lane. Go left down this the short way to a gate onto the head of a surfaced road. Descend this through the edge of Bradley, going left as College Road out onto a through road in the village. Turn right to the shop corner then left along the street. *At the end, a detour left before the sports fields will take you to the Slaters Arms.* Continuing straight on between sports fields and the former mill you soon arrive at a swing bridge on the canal. Cross and go left on the towpath which will return you to the start.

Features of interest en route include a Polish war memorial at Hamblethorpe swing bridge. *It pays tribute to the seven crew of a Wellington bomber from RAF Skipton-on-Swale killed in a 1943 crash.* Further on you encounter Farnhill Wood with its springtime bluebell carpet; views back to the monument; Farnhill Bridge, and canal milestones. *Across a loop of the canal Farnhill Hall's dark turrets peer through the trees, dating in part from the 14th century.* Near the end Farnhill's canalside buildings are on parade before crossing the village street on an aqueduct to conclude.

SUTTON CLOUGH

WALK 9

Colourful surrounds, steep slopes and a deep wooded dell

START Sutton-in-Craven (SE 005441; BD20 7LP)

DISTANCE 5 miles (8km)

ORDNANCE SURVEY 1:25,000 MAP
Explorer OL21 - South Pennines

ACCESS Start from the village centre. Roadside parking. Keighley-Skipton bus

Sutton is a sizeable village in the shadow of steep hills, and is dominated by its large mill buildings, now residential. The older High Street area has some fine old cottages. The public park, three pubs, shops and a chip shop add further benefits. From the main junction outside the park, with the Black Bull to your right, follow the High Street left. Keep left to a fork just before the beck, and as West Lane goes right, take the unsigned road straight ahead at Harper Square. This is Hall Drive, which runs as a suburban street beyond an impressive arch. *The double lodge here belonged to long-demolished Sutton Hall.* Beyond the houses a footbridge takes the ensuing broad way into the trees of Sutton Clough.

Keep on the main way with Lumb Clough Beck on your right, passing arched bridge, footbridge and concrete bridge before then succumbing to a tiny footbridge. Ignoring the firmer path rising right, a path traces the opposite bank upstream to reach a beautiful

WALK 9 • SUTTON CLOUGH

confluence, then begins to climb. Enjoy lovely waterplay as the often muddy path climbs between boulders. *The enormous Gater Stone hangs above the steep slopes opposite, while springtime offers a nice bluebell display.* The path remains near the beck in its wooded ravine until it turns to climb steeply and more firmly away. Here leave it, and advance a few strides to the stream before crossing to the opposite bank. A few strides further upstream, a good path doubles back up the slope to the left to a stile out of the clough. Turn right up the field towards Wood Top Farm.

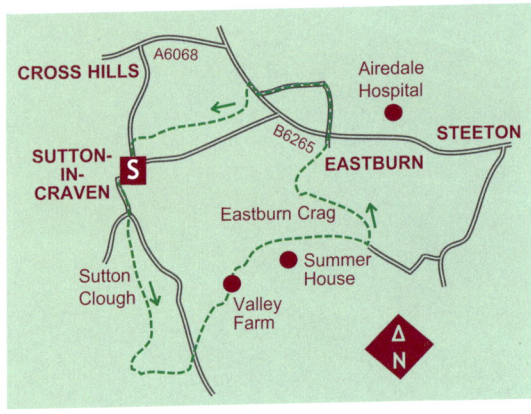

From a stile to its left, an enclosed path curves left outside the grounds to a ladder-stile by a stone hut. *The first open views look up-dale to Farnhill Moor and beyond.* Descend the wallside to a stile on the left into a sidestream's wooded confines. *An attractive little fall tumbles over a rocky ledge immediately upstream.* Heading downstream, within fifty paces a less obvious, part-stepped path drops down to cross the beck, and on a short way to a stile back out. Contour round the steeply sloping field above the trees to find an intriguing stile with steps down the other side. *This is a pleasant corner above the limits of yet another branch of the wooded clough.* Rise through rampant hollies to a hidden stile at the top, then shadow the wallside up to neighbouring stiles onto an access road. *Views look out over Sutton and Glusburn and higher up the Aire Valley.* Go left through the farm and out onto a road.

SUTTON CLOUGH • WALK 9

Cross straight over to Long House, behind which a brief walled way leads out into a field. *Massive views include Sutton Clough, Cowling Tower, the Malhamdale hills of Rye Loaf Hill and Kirkby Fell, Fountains Fell, Flasby Fell and Barden Moor.* Cross the field to a gate, aiming for Valley Farm ahead. Pass beneath a tiny stone hut to locate a stile in the facing wall. Advance on a faint trod through rougher pasture to a far corner wall-stile, then rise left to a gate into the yard at Valley Farm. Pass straight through and out via a gate onto a walled green way. Emerging into a field cross to a stile to the right of some communications masts, and then on to bridle-gates through a sliver of woodland. Advance through a gate ahead, then bear right to a corner gate onto the driveway serving Summer House.

Head away on the long, gently declining drive. *Big views look across to Silsden beneath Rombalds Moor.* Just before a bend where it becomes surfaced as Intake Lane, take a gate on the left from where the grassy wallside track of Moor Lane drops away. *Fine views up the valley feature Cross Hills, Kildwick, Farnhill Moor, Flasby Fell and into the heart of the Dales. Immediately to the left of the path are spread the modest boulders of Eastburn Crag.* A delightful enclosed section leads down to colourful country around Eastburn's old quarries. The path slants down well above the quarry, and curves down the other side as it broadens. *After a second seat on a knoll a short-cut path drops more directly down.*

The track becomes an access road, dropping down, now paved, into Eastburn by the Post office/shop. Eastburn is a tiny village that sprang to prominence when the sprawling Airedale Hospital was built in 1970 between here and neighbouring Steeton. *Its pub is the Inn at Eastburn, formerly the White Bear (and for a spell the Nightingale) just further along to the left.* Take advantage of a pedestrian crossing over the main road, then go left a few strides to escape down Green Lane. At the bottom turn left on Lyon Road to rejoin the main road. Cross and go right, leaving by a surfaced path immediately after crossing Holme Beck at Eastburn Bridge. *Ahead is the Earl Crag skyline, with a wild garlic carpeted wood to your left.* This firm path shadows the beck upstream all the way back to Sutton. Ignoring a footbridge/setted ford part way along, remain on a good path to join the road at a bridge. Turn left and conclude through the park.

WALK 10
EARL CRAG

Lovely beck scenery contrasts with a gritstone escarpment supporting two follies and giving breathtaking views

START Cowling (SD 967430; BD22 0DD)

DISTANCE 6¼ miles (10km)

ORDNANCE SURVEY 1:25,000 MAP
Explorer OL21 - South Pennines

ACCESS *Start from Cowling parish church at Ickornshaw, at west end of village just off A6068. Roadside parking. Keighley-Colne/Burnley bus on main road.*

Cowling is a windswept gritstone mill community, indeed a classic Pennine example. Its rows of dark terraces are strung along the length of the village, on or close to the main road 'over the moss' to Lancashire. Here are the Bay Horse pub and several main street shops. 19th century Holy Trinity church stands aloof in the older part of the village, with a former Sunday School by the church gate. Nearby is the house where famous son Philip Snowden, an early 20th century Chancellor of the Exchequer, was born. From the church gate take the road opposite, through the hamlet of Ickornshaw. *On your right is the converted Methodist Chapel of 1876, which closed in 1985.* Immediately after crossing Ickornshaw Beck, a stone-stepped path climbs steeply left to the main road. *On your right is the former Black Bull pub.*

EARL CRAG • WALK 10

Go briefly left on the footway and cross to a small gate opposite. A faint path ascends the field, passing through an intervening gate and easing out to cross to a small gate in the wall ahead. On your right is the mullioned windowed Lower Summer House. Through the gate bear right up above poultry pens above the farm to the foot of a rising walled green way. *Cowling Pinnacle perches on the edge of Earl Crag over to the left, while Pendle Hill appears far to the west.* Easing out, it merges into the rough access road of Lumb Lane alongside a modern barn. Advance straight on as far as a gate. *Though the route doesn't pass through, it is worth doing so to see a little waterfall at close hand on Lumb Head Beck.*

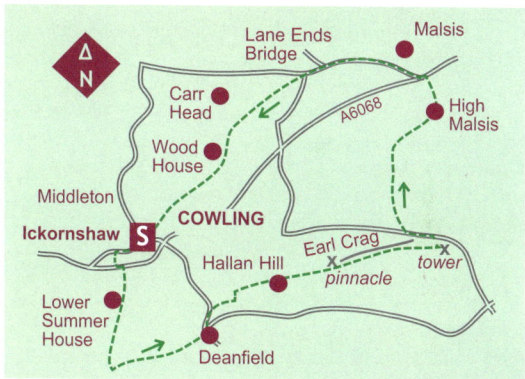

The onward route takes a gate on the left, from where a part sunken way descends Wool Hey Brow by the wall. *Big views look over this side valley of Dean Hole Clough to Wainman's Pinnacle, with extensive moorland to the right.* At the bottom Lumb Head Beck is crossed and the path runs on by trees to a gate in front of the main beck. Across, the walled track of Close Lane scales the opposite slope to emerge onto the sharp bend of a narrow road at Deanfield.

Turn left just as far as Court House Farm on the right. Enter the yard and pass the house to a gate/gap out into the field behind. A thin path follows the wall away to the very end, where a small gate above a small wooded clough admits onto a broad green way. Go left just thirty paces to its tapering demise at another such gate. Through this, climb the steep bank on the right. *The Cowling*

WALK 10 • EARL CRAG

scene is well presented below, the entire village laid out end to end. The slope eases to reveal Wainman's Pinnacle beckoning much closer now, beyond the farm at Hallan Hill.

Advance straight up the fields with an old wall on the right. Through the top field centre a stile admits into the farm. Keep left of the buildings to follow the drive up onto the open moor of Cludders. As the drive turns sharp right, a broad path bears left towards what proves to be a distinct edge - be aware of an old quarry rim here. *To the south a big sweep of moorland looks to the Hitching Stone above Stott Hill Moor and Ickornshaw Moor.* A broad old way that surmounts the quarried edge now rises gently up above broken gritstone outcrops to the waiting Pinnacle.

Earl Crag is a mile-long gritstone outcrop which dominates the skyline of South Craven. Atop it, a long half-mile apart, are its two occupants sometimes dubbed the 'salt & pepper pots'. It is only at this point that Lund's Tower is revealed at the far end. Built on solid rock, the Pinnacle dates from the early 19th century and is better known as Cowling Pinnacle. The panorama is both extensive and absorbing: many local features draw the eye beyond the rim, including Farnhill Moor, Pinhaw Beacon, Skipton Moor, Rombalds Moor, and villages such as Cross Hills, Bradley and Kildwick.

The promenade along the crest of Earl Crag to Lund's Tower is a local favourite, and is as obvious as it looks. After the second of two kissing-gates in sturdy walls, things open out into a broad greensward, and an iron kissing-gate in a fence heralds arrival at the tower. *Built by James Lund and known locally as Cowling Tower or Sutton Pinnacle, its grassy base is set back from an old quarry. It boasts 39 spiral steps up to a small platform from which to survey the exhilarating vista extending far into the Yorkshire Dales. The drop of the quarry exaggerates the airiness!*

Leave the tower by a path from the fence, which circumvents the cliff on concrete steps to drop down onto a road. Turn down this just as far as a gate at the drive to the derelict house at Brush on the right. *Earl Crag now presents a jagged skyline above.* Ignoring the drive, descend half-left to a gate, below which is a short enclosed way. From a stile at the end follow the wall on your left down through a succession of fields, eventually reaching a gate from where the wall and route swing right to a corner gate. A track runs the short way to High Malsis. Don't enter the farmyard but take a gate/stile just below to reach a short row of houses. Here an access road descends to the A6068. The Dog & Gun pub is just two minutes to the right. *Over the road stands Malsis, a large house that from 1920 to 2014 was an independent school.*

Cross to the footway opposite and go left to the junction. Take the side road (Carr Head Lane) for a leisurely ten minutes, over Lumb Mill Bridge and passing Lumb Mill House and Lumb Mill Farm. *The skyline to the left features the crest of Earl Crag.* Just beyond a branch right, leave by one to the left. The road quickly descends to Lane Ends Bridge. Immediately over it, re-cross Lumb Mill Beck on a footbridge and cross to a flight of stones steps. At the top of the bank the path turns left to begin a delightful ramble, closing in on the beck. You initially pass a small pond and then a very well-preserved limekiln in the park-like surroundings of Carr Head Hall. *There is an early glimpse of the house up to the right.*

Immediately past the confluence of Ickornshaw Beck and Gill Beck is Ridge Mill Bridge on the latter. *This bridle-bridge of 2011 replaced one destroyed by a fallen tree, while a previous stone-arched bridge was swept away in 1967.* Across it follow a broad path bearing away right to run briefly above the beck. At a track junction just around the corner beneath isolated Wood House, bear right up past the house on the green byway of Cinder Hill Lane. This leads unerringly back - high above Ickornshaw Beck - to broaden into a firm track at a barnyard, ultimately emerging by the church.

Looking north from Earl Crag

WALK 11
DOUBLER STONES

A lengthy climb to gain peerless views over Wharfedale

START Silsden (SE 041464; BD20 0PA)

DISTANCE 6½ miles (10½km)

ORDNANCE SURVEY 1:25,000 MAP
Explorer OL21 - South Pennines

ACCESS Start from the centre, car park opposite church.
Bus from Keighley and Ilkley, railway station a mile distant.

Silsden is a busy town with much modern housing, originally a mill community retaining many terraced streets. Its main street, Kirkgate, has numerous pubs, shops and cafes. Head south along Kirkgate to the Leeds-Liverpool Canal. Across, turn left down onto the towpath and head away east. Finally entering open countryside, cross Hainsworth Road at Brunthwaite swing bridge and continue to Holden swing bridge. This time cross the bridge and follow the enclosed track to Howden Park Farm and out onto Holden Lane.

Turning right, the road commences a punishingly steep climb. When it bends sharp right, take a gate in front and follow an access track the short way to a modern barn. As the track drops left, take a gate in front and follow the grassy way rising gently ahead. From the second small gate in the adjacent fence a grassy path heads away, slanting down through colourful surroundings to the deep rim of Holden Beck. It then traces the rim uphill, soon reaching a fork:

DOUBLER STONES • WALK 11

here you can drop left down stone steps into a ravine secreting a waterfall. The onward path rises to run inside the wood top, crossing a sidestream with a small waterfall to a corner stile behind. The path heads away beneath gorse bushes to join a track. This drops through a gate to a ford/footbridge beneath an aqueduct. *This is the former Bradford Corporation's pipeline from the Nidderdale reservoirs.*

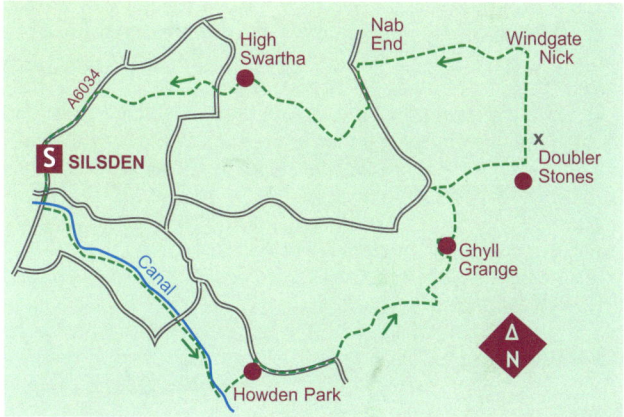

The track heads away towards a wall: ignore the stile and turn up the nearside to a gate in a recess near the top. An enclosed grass track rises away to Ghyll Grange Farm. Remain on the track which runs left outside the perimeter: at a junction with the access road turn right over a cattle-grid and into the yard. *Over a century ago visitors to the charms of Holden Gill found refreshment at the farm - though large parties required two days notice.* Remain on the concrete track rising left past the house. Just beyond a modern house on your right, leave the access road for an enclosed grassy cart track climbing left. From a gate at the top follow the wall on your left away, tapering to meet another farm road just short of a road. Double back right on the concrete road which rises to a gate, then on two minutes further to Doubler Stones Farm.

Just after a bungalow turn left up a thin path onto the moor, running below the weirdly weathered Doubler Stones. Beyond a kissing-gate in a fence the path runs on into heather, rising gently to a boundary wall along the crest of Rombalds Moor. Just a minute

WALK 11 • DOUBLER STONES

further comes the walk's highlight, arrival at a cairn at Windgate Nick, bringing Wharfedale spectacularly into the scene. *Beneath your feet old quarries fall away towards the farms of Addingham Moorside. Bolton Abbey, Simon's Seat and Beamsley Beacon are prominent, with Barden Moor leading the eye to the Wharfedale mountains of Buckden Pike and Great Whernside. Rombalds Moor stretches far above Ilkley.*

Turn left along the escarpment, passing a memorial stone. *This recalls two crewmen of a de Haviland Mosquito from RAF Church Fenton killed in a crash in March 1943.* Quickly rejoining the wall at a stile which you ignore, as sunken ways turn downhill, remain on a wallside path to a corner stile. Go left outside White Crag Plantation to Nab End. *A massive Aire Valley prospect is revealed: below are Silsden and its reservoir, the silvery line of the Leeds-Liverpool Canal, and Earl Crag with a more distant Pendle Hill beyond.* The path drops past minor rocks to a stile onto Lightbank Lane.

Go left beneath White Crag for a couple of minutes to a gate on the right. An old green way descends a wallside, through a gateway then bears right to a gate in the bottom corner onto an access road in front of cottages at North End Farm. Cross to a small gate in front, and down a little slope to the lower house. Just to its left is a wall-stile into a field below, where drop to a wall-stile below. Now bear right down a sloping pasture, through a gap-stile on a bend and slant again to the bottom corner. Bridging Brunthwaite Beck, rise through a gate/stile on a wallside grassy way over the brow to a gate/stile revealing High Swartha Farm below.

Drop down onto the track just below, and go right a few strides on it to a stile in the adjacent wall. Through this double back left down a tapering enclosure to a couple of small gates onto the access road. Descend this to join Swartha Lane. Cross to a gate opposite and bear left off the short Haw Farm drive, a grassy path curving round beneath gorse bushes to a corner with kissing-gate and wall-stile. A snicket path then drops down to emerge into a field in front. Head straight down the left side of the fence, through a stile in the bottom corner and down again to a small gate in a wall-stile on the right. Turn right on the enclosed path down the edge of some allotments to emerge onto Bolton Road at Town Head on the edge of Silsden. Go left down the footway back into the centre.

ALDER CARR WOOD

WALK 12

Easy walking by towpath to woodland and farmland

START *Riddlesden (SE 079422; BD21 4HD)*

DISTANCE *6 miles (9½km)*

ORDNANCE SURVEY 1:25,000 MAP
Explorer OL21 - South Pennines **or**
Explorer 297 - Lower Wharfedale & Washburn Valley

ACCESS *Start from near East Riddlesden Hall on B6265 Bradford Road. Roadside parking. Keighley-Bradford/Leeds bus.*

Riddlesden is a suburban community famous for East Riddlesden Hall, a splendid house of 1642 built by Halifax clothier James Murgatroyd. It sits in lovely grounds overlooking the River Aire: in the care of the National Trust, it is open to visitors. Contrastingly hidden amid modern suburbia on Scott Lane is West Riddlesden Hall, a fine manor house of 1687 that is a private residence. From the traffic lights turn the short way up Granby Lane to the swing bridge on the Leeds-Liverpool Canal, with the Marquis of Granby pub opposite. Don't cross but turn left on the towpath, quickly arriving at another swing bridge at Bar Lane. *Bar Lane is so named from the tollhouse that existed at the junction with Bradford Road until its demolition in the 1960s: just to your left is a Post office/shop.*

Cross and resume on the towpath, whose surfaced course heads away past a red-brick former warehouse and on for some

WALK 12 • ALDER CARR WOOD

time with housing opposite. Just beyond a milestone is Leach's swing bridge. The walk will return to this point, but for now simply trace the initially tarmac towpath which quickly transforms back into a proper path after some scattered houses on the left.

A splendid stride ensues, with Low Wood on the opposite bank and views over the valley with sightings of the Aire below. Keighley golf course comes in on your left, and another milestone is passed just before Booths swing bridge. *Here a broad path drops left to detour a few strides to view an old limekiln below the canal. This is a splendid structure with a massive outer arch and an internal one too, probably dating from the arrival of the canal some two centuries ago.* The towpath marches on, the wood finally ends and the canal curves round to Lower Holden Farm. Passing beneath Lodge Hill Bridge, the surface downgrades to grass as you march grandly on through open countryside. *Big views look over the valley, with Silsden ahead and White Crag ahead to the right: Spring Crag and Alder Carr Woods are set back just to the right.* Before long you arrive at Holden swing bridge, the turning point of the walk. Cross the bridge and follow the walled track to Howden Park Farm.

Entering the yard, turn sharp right on a walled cart track. At the end the track takes the right-hand of two gates to continue along a wallside. Through an intervening gate it runs on to end at a corner gate. Bear left up the open field to a stile into Alder Carr Wood. The path rises away to the right, a sustained pull easing out at a pylon. Rising more gently it soon reaches a broader track. Go straight across, rising again to almost at once cross another such

ALDER CARR WOOD • WALK 12

track before rising a few feet further to a wall-stile into a field. Head away, joining a faint grassy track and rising gently across a boulder-strewn pasture to a gate in the wall ahead. Continue rising to a gate beneath Jaytail Farm, but don't pass through. Instead bear right along the field top, passing a spring to a corner stile. A smashing path heads away, running beneath the wall along the part wooded top of this extensive sloping pasture. *Below is the former Riddlesden golf course, closed in 2016 as a result of dwindling membership. Big views look over Keighley and up the Worth Valley.*

A super path runs all the way to a small gate at the end. Cross little Clough Beck and rise gently away, crossing the field bottom to a gate above a modern house. Advance to the drive just ahead, and follow its level course out: shortly another drive merges from High Wood Head to the right. Here take a hand-gate on the right and descend the wallside to Low Wood Head. A stile at the bottom sends an enclosed path along between the hamlet's houses into a yard. Advance straight on the driveway out, quickly slanting down to become more enclosed as the fields end. Here take an easily missed hand-gate on the right, and descend the field outside a deep wooded gill to a similar gate at the bottom. A briefly enclosed path drops past a house onto an access road.

Go briefly left to cross the gill, and on the edge of suburbia at Western Avenue take a path down the other side of the ravine, a few wooden steps pointing the path down onto another access road at the bottom. Cross straight over and down a broad, enclosed way onto yet another access road in front of an odd mix of houses. Turn left, and as Leach Road this quickly joins the canal bank to return to Leach's Bridge. Cross to rejoin the towpath and retrace opening steps to the start.

At East Riddlesden Hall

WALK 13: NEWSHOLME DEAN

A walk of immense variety and colour, from moorland heights to a steep, wooded valley of great character

START Slippery Ford (SE 002403; BD22 0QE)

DISTANCE 7 miles ($11^{1}4$km)

ORDNANCE SURVEY 1:25,000 MAP
Explorer OL21 - South Pennines

ACCESS *Start from a parking area at Morkin Bridge, on Whitehill Road 2 miles north-west of Oakworth.*

Leave the parking area on a surfaced drive climbing to the house at Higher Intake. Through the gate beyond you enter Keighley Moor, and the road ascends past a large boulder to shortly arrive at the embankment of Keighley Moor Reservoir. *Built in the 1830s to supply water to local mills, it is locally known as 'The Big Dam'.* Cross the grassy embankment to a fork fifty yards beyond the end. While a broader way swings right, take the left branch, gliding gently down through the heather of Oakworth Moor. *Ahead is a wide Bronte skyline, with the moorland horizon reaching from Ovenden Moor windfarm round to Crow Hill.* An early moist spell is best evaded on its left, before the path settles down to a pleasant stroll with a line of grouse butts just to the right. Alongside an old boundary stone a wall comes in for company, and after 150 yards you reach a gateway in it.

NEWSHOLME DEAN • WALK 13

Pass through onto another path heading away. In a gentle groove, it bears right to pass between shooting butts, then veers left on a slight rise to a brow. Across this an equally gentle descent drops down another groove to meet a surfaced access road leaving the moor. Pass through gate, stile or cattle-grid, and head away along the enclosed Broad Head Lane. It drops steadily down, its middle section being unsurfaced but still firm, passing Broad Head Farm to finally arrive at a junction.

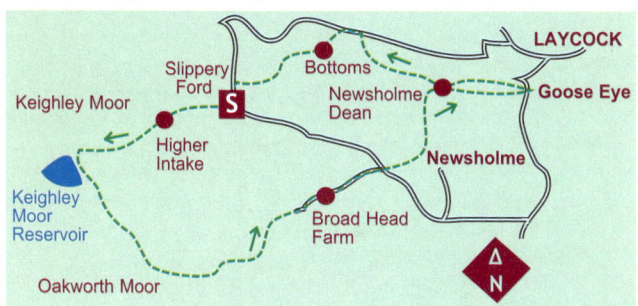

Cross straight over along a driveway, which immediately bears right to a house, but you keep on the enclosed cart track straight ahead. This drops to a sharp bend right, where you leave it. *Two minutes along the track to the right is the hamlet of Newsholme. At its heart is Church Farm, which in an intriguing architectural and spiritual arrangement stands semi-detached with a church. Linked to Oakworth parish, St John's church was constructed in 1840. The old farm bears a 1670 datestone, and both boast arch-headed mullioned windows.* From a gateway on the left a gentler enclosed grassy way runs the short way along to a bridle-gate at the head of Cat Clough, overlooking Newsholme Dean.

The path immediately undertakes a steep descent of Cat Clough. *This colourful wooded cleft is your gateway into the charms of Newsholme Dean.* Head straight down, crossing the diverted streamlet and down through scrub to a gate. Cross the field to a choice of bridges on Dean Beck. *Alongside the arched farm bridge is a splendid old slab bridge, one of its four great blocks being oddly superfluous.* Across, head away to a gate in the corner just ahead. An enclosed track rises the very short way to the

WALK 13 • NEWSHOLME DEAN

first of the cottages of Newsholme Dean. Follow the access road on past a couple more dwellings, and it soon begins a concerted climb out of the valley. Part way up, at the last house, note the grassy cart track doubling back from a gate on the left: this is the onward route after a loop to incorporate Goose Eye. *Omitting Goose Eye would save a good half-hour, more if sampling its hospitality.*

The full route advances a few yards further, where go right on a narrow path above the house. Just beyond its grounds, take the right fork to slant down, part flagged, then running on above an open field. Soon reaching a walled corner at the end, it drops flagged again into the top corner of a wood. Resuming, ignore the right branch down to a footbridge, and remain on the splendid upper level path. This soon arrives at an attractive millpond in greenery. Just beyond it a wooden footbridge crosses the old cut, and the path resumes in the company of the lively beck, passing a weir. At the end a footbridge crosses it and a gap-stile puts you onto a road. Go left to enter Goose Eye.

Goose Eye is a former industrial hamlet sheltering in its own deep hollow, focal point being the popular Turkey Inn. Its modern history sprang into life in the late 1970s, with the opening of a tiny brewery in an old mill building where paper for banknotes was once made. Though the venture ceased after ten years, it was revived in Keighley in 1991 to the delight of discerning drinkers. By way of a remarkable coincidence, the pub's next owner restored brewing to the hamlet, so for several years the confusing result was that Turkey beers were brewed in Goose Eye, and Goose Eye beers brewed in Keighley (which they still are).

Continue a short way beyond the pub, leaving by the rough access road of Lund Lane on the left before the steep hill. Ignoring a driveway rising left, advance past several houses on the right. In trees beyond them, the track turns sharp left up towards the house at Brow End Farm. Keep right on a narrower path outside its grounds, running a splendid enclosed course around and gently up to Newsholme Dean's access road. Bear left, briefly descending then enjoying an extended level section with good views over the valley. At the end it drops down the short way to encounter the earlier route in Newsholme Dean.

Leave the access road at the first building where the gate on the right sends a cart track along to another gate. Bear right on the

NEWSHOLME DEAN • WALK 13

inviting ascending green way, and after crossing a streamlet remain on the path alongside the upper, sunken way. *All around is the splendid relative wilderness of Newsholme Dean.* Above an old quarry a flagged section begins, rising to a gate and resuming, still flagged up to a bend. Continue up this paved way, which as it swings away from the Dean rises in sunken fashion between heathery verges. Levelling out, it passes through a gate onto Greystones Lane.

Just fifty paces along to the left, head back towards the Dean on an access road slanting down to Bottoms Farm. Entering the yard take a small gate set back on the right, crossing a field bottom to a corner stile beyond a barn. Across a streamlet in colourful surrounds the path runs round to the left, contouring the slope to open out into a clearing. Bear slightly left on a thin path to a stile/gate above a wood. Now cross a couple of fields linked by wall-stiles beneath a house at Greystones. The third field is rough moor-grass, and a thin path heads away slightly left, dropping through a gateway in an old wall and down again to a confluence of tree-lined becks. Cross the right branch to a gate behind, and follow the left side of the field before ascending a wallside to the farm of Slitheroford (formerly Near Slippery Ford). Pass through the gate and on between farm buildings out onto narrow Slippery Ford Lane. Turn left back to Morkin Bridge, passing a stone trough inscribed 1852.

Newsholme Dean

WALK 14
PONDEN CLOUGH

An invigorating exploration of Ponden's scenic surrounds

START *Oldfield (SE 006381; BD22 0RX)*

DISTANCE *5^3⁄4 miles (9^1⁄4km)*

ORDNANCE SURVEY 1:25,000 MAP
Explorer OL21 - South Pennines

ACCESS *Start from a moorland parking area at Hare Hill Edge above Oldfield, 200 yards west of Grouse Inn.*

Head west along the Colne road away from the Grouse, with extensive views over Stanbury to the Bronte moors. Just before the moor ends, turn left down a walled path past a water treatment works. At the bottom you emerge onto a road between a tiny school and a row of cottages in Oldfield. Turn left, and just past the school turn right down a short access road. *This serves several houses that form the nucleus of the hamlet. On the left is Oldfield House with mullioned windows, dating from the 17th century.*

At the bottom turn sharp right on a drive, keeping on to the end where advance on a few paces over the lawn to a corner stile into a field. Follow the fence away to another stile, from where a fenced path advances on above Oldfield End Farm onto its drive. Cross to a gate ahead and follow the left-hand boundary to a corner kissing-gate. *Ponden Reservoir appears ahead, backed by Ponden Clough itself.* Now commence a sustained slant left, down to a gate/kissing-gate in a fence, down through a gate in the fence

PONDEN CLOUGH • WALK 14

below, then down to stiles in successive descending walls. A little path then drops left in a scrubby hollow, quickly swinging right to run with a fence in the valley bottom. Just before the corner a stile puts you alongside the River Worth. Turn right over a streamlet slab bridge to a stile onto Hob Lane alongside a road bridge.

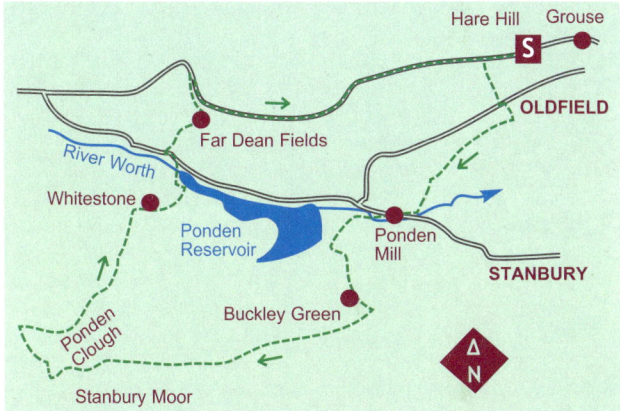

Cross straight over and along the firm access road opposite, passing Ponden Mill. *A café operates at the derelict mill, which in recent times was a popular retail outlet.* Running parallel with the Worth, the road bridges it then climbs to arrive alongside the dam of Ponden Reservoir. Here turn sharp left up the enclosed Pennine Way track rising away, past the old farm of Rush Isles and climbing as a grand path to a bridle-gate at Buckley House.

Follow the drive rising left to a junction at a couple of houses at Buckley Green Bottom. *At Buckley Green lived Timmy Feather, who died in 1910 and is remembered as the last of the handloom weavers.* Double sharply back right here on a stony access road along the base of moorland to end at a house at Far Slack. Don't enter but bear left on a path running the few strides to a kissing-gate in a fence onto the edge of Stanbury Moor. An excellent path heads away above the wall, rising gently through bilberries in delectable surroundings. Down below is the reservoir, while directly ahead is Ponden Clough, with its lower reaches well-wooded, a riot of colour culminating abruptly where two tumbling becks merge.

WALK 14 • PONDEN CLOUGH

As the wall parts company the path continues across the moor, levelling out for a super stride more closely above the edge of the steeper drop, with an improving view of the clough. This leads to Middle Moor Clough, first of the two feeder streams. Dropping to cross a simple bridge, ignore a steep path down into the clough and resume on the main path rising very briefly left. Double sharply back right to head around the rim of the clough, soon arriving above the rocky outcrop of Ponden Kirk. *As the Penistone Crag of 'Wuthering Heights', it requires little imagination to visualise this backdrop to Cathy's and Heathcliff's tormented story: beneath the crag is the natural aperture to which Cathy makes reference. Legend tells that should a maid undertake the crawl through this dark, grimy orifice, she shall be married within the year.*

The path continues round to cross the northern feeder stream, a lovely spot, then swings back right to leave the clough along its rim. Dropping to a crumbling wall corner, don't pass through but remain left of the wall, a thin path dropping down its side towards a restored house at Upper Ponden. At a path junction just before its wall bear left, crossing two tracks coming out from the house and continuing down a thin but clear path to meet a firm green track. Cross straight over on a thin trod to a ladder-stile in the wall just below. Leaving the moor, resume down a crumbling wallside. At another old gateway turn right along the rear of the house at Whitestone to a ladder-stile, and on a walled green way to a stile onto another such way. Turn left down this, dropping as a track around the head of Ponden Reservoir, and merging into a driveway for the final yards (bridging the reservoir head) onto a road.

Go very briefly left and take a stile on the right. Ascend by an old wall to a stile in a recess at the top, and up two further field-sides to houses above. Turn left at the top corner to pass through a small gate beneath the top house (Far Dean Fields) to join its drive. This rises steeply away, and above a few pines and before a sharp bend left, take a level path contouring left across newly planted slopes. *This enjoys good views into the uppermost Worth Valley.* Through a second small gate it runs on above wooded Dean Clough to emerge via a gate onto a road. Double back right on this to return to the start. This half-hour road walk is a lovely near level stride, initially beneath moorland and with big views over the Worth Valley, and initially Ponden Reservoir.

TOP WITHINS

WALK 15

A literary pilgrimage to a celebrated moorland landmark

START Haworth (SE 018362; BD22 9RE)

DISTANCE 6¼ miles (10km)

ORDNANCE SURVEY 1:25,000 MAP
Explorer OL21 - South Pennines

ACCESS Start from Penistone Hill car park on Oxenhope-Stanbury road (Moor Side Lane) a mile west of village.

Penistone Hill has changed from man's workshop to his playground, its former quarries now car parks for the leisure seeker. Most of the numerous guideposts over the next hour or so feature Japanese, an indication of the fascination for the Brontes with students from the Land of the Rising Sun. Good views look over the Worth Valley to the settlements of Oldfield and Oakworth, and back over Keighley to Rombalds Moor. Rejoin unfenced Moor Side Lane on the north side of the brow. *On the brow itself, just up to the left, is Tom Stell's Seat, a gritstone block of 1932 recalling a local rambler 'who loved these moors'.*

Crossing straight over the road, a path runs the short way to a kissing-gate in a fence and heads away across Haworth Moor. *Immediate views look over the valley to Stanbury: note the parallel walls dropping down from the village towards largely hidden Lower Laithe Reservoir. The Bronte moorlands fill the skyline ahead,*

WALK 15 • TOP WITHINS

from Withins Height round to Wycoller Ark. After an early moist section a good path enjoys a grand stroll across the moor, bearing very gently right to ultimately merge into a firm wallside track.

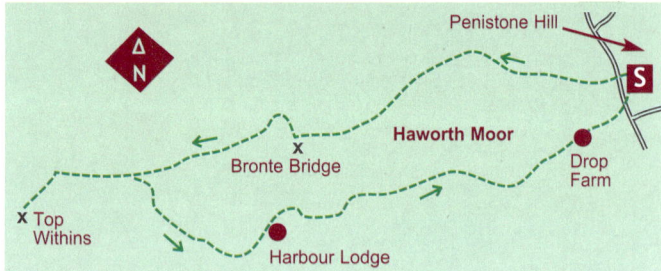

Continue along this past the ruin of Far Intake, narrowing into a broad path as the moor opens out. *The isolated farmstead of Harbour Lodge is seen ahead beneath the Top Withins skyline, whose attendant trees aid identification as they just break the horizon.* To your right is the colourful side valley of South Dean Beck, into which you are about to descend. The wall drops away and your now rougher path runs down and on to arrive at Bronte Bridge, a simple but attractive footbridge. *By the path before it is the seat-shaped stone known as the Bronte Chair, while another boulder carries a plaque with a biblical quote. A stone tablet by the bridge records its re-building in 1990 following flash floods.*

Across the bridge take the steep, partly stepped path climbing directly away, through an old wall to quickly reach a kissing-gate in a fence. Here the path forks; go left, slanting up, part flagged, through old walls to reach a sturdy wall. The path now runs left on a sustained level stroll parallel with the beck down to the left. Through a gap-stile at the end you then pass along the base of an unexpected lush sheep pasture, and at the end a kissing-gate puts you back onto true moorland. The left-hand wall drops away and your path runs grandly on, with Top Withins directly ahead and not so distant now.

Just before the path curves right to stepping-stones on a side-stream, note a guidepost sending a thinner path doubling back sharply left: this will be your return route. For now keep on to a confluence, across which you commence a part-flagged climb

TOP WITHINS • WALK 15

towards Top Withins. The path meets the flagged Pennine Way at the meagre ruin of Withins. Turn left for two minutes rising gently to the justifiably more celebrated Top Withins. *Top Withins, or simply 'Withins' (as Withins and Lower Withins are now only piles of stones), is a famous ruin where one requires solitude in order to imbibe the atmosphere. A small shelter in a dingy outhouse and an array of outdoor seating all contribute to the demise of any 'wild' feeling. Top Withins is regarded as the Earnshaw home in Emily's classic 'Wuthering Heights'. It is difficult to imagine that this lonely outpost was once a home, but whether or not Emily Bronte actually visualised Heathcliff here, one can readily imagine her story being enacted in this bleak and inhospitable moorland setting which is, indeed, 'wuthering'.*

Retrace steps to the guidepost shortly after the streamlet, and bear right on a lesser, level path between the main path and the stream. This quickly arrives at a pair of adjacent footbridges. Across the second on Crumber Dike, the path ascends the bank of the sidestream, soon easing to run grandly on through heather atop the bank. As the clough fades, the path runs on alongside a reedy hollow, reaching a path junction guidepost. Keep straight on through this neat little pass, soon revealing open views ahead to Haworth Moor and part of Leeshaw Reservoir from a grassy terrace above the hollow. The path swings left to reveal the isolated farm of Harbour Lodge just below. Passing left of its confines the path concludes through a briefly moist section to join another path. Turn right over a small footbridge, above which is the farm's access road. *Just above is a memorial to a moorland gamekeeper.*

Turn left away from the farm, and on for some time until beyond an appreciable kink. As the road levels and straightens, it is seen for some distance ahead as it crosses the moor. Advance on (further than the map suggests) until a minor brow, with the straight, flat road running on. Here a marker post sends a thin but clear path slanting off to the right. This angles gently down, and after an early moist section it greatly improves to merge with a wall along the bottom of the moor. A good path is joined to run along to the left. After a gentle rise Penistone Hill re-appears ahead, with Drop Farm (occasional refreshments) en route. Keep straight on along its drive to the road, then left back up onto Penistone Hill.

WALK 16
WORTH VALLEY

A wealth of interest including two packhorse bridges

START *Haworth (SE 034372; BD22 8NJ)*

DISTANCE *5¼ miles (8½km)*

ORDNANCE SURVEY 1:25,000 MAP
Explorer OL21 - South Pennines

ACCESS *Start from the railway station. Car parks nearby. Bus and Worth Valley train from Keighley.*

Haworth ceased to be just another village in the 19th century when the fame of the Brontes spread, and for several decades has been a full-blown tourist honeypot. Focal point is the main street, lined with shops and cafes unashamedly aimed at visitors. Despite a by-pass the street still resounds to the bustle of cars nudging pedestrians from its setts. The street climbs steeply to St Michael's church, surrounded by pubs. Only its tower would be recognisable to the Brontes, the rest having been rebuilt around 1880. Inside, the Bronte Vault holds the remains of all but Anne, whose grave overlooks the sea at Scarborough. It is said some 40,000 villagers are at rest in Haworth churchyard. Behind the church is the elegant Georgian parsonage of 1779, and just across a cobbled side street is the school where the Bronte siblings taught. The parsonage is now a museum of its former occupants, the spiritual heart of the Bronte scene. Haworth is the world's first Fairtrade village.

WORTH VALLEY • WALK 16

Haworth station is home to the village's other major attraction, the steam railway which celebrates its 50th anniversary as this book is published (see page 62). From the station take the adjacent footbridge over the railway, and rise left a few strides on Belle Isle Road to the foot of setted Butt Lane. *On the right is a three-storey weaver's cottage, with Lower Mill Hill Farm on the left.* Ascend the broad, very steep road to Rawdon Road at the top. *A nicer alternative takes an early gateway on the left to meander up through Central Park to rejoin Butt Lane at the top.* Cross straight over and up a little road finishing in a few cobbles onto the Main Street opposite the Fleece Inn. Turn right up the street to where it levels out at the church gates.

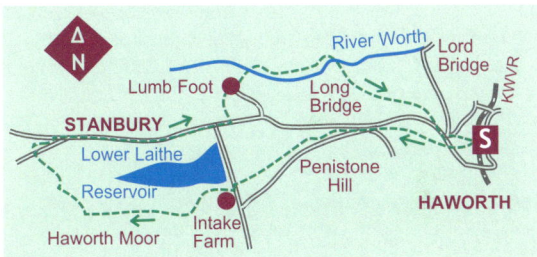

Ascend the steps and pass right of the church onto a setted road. This rises past the churchyard and former school to Bronte Parsonage. Just past it an enclosed path takes over, running between fields and housing to emerge at the end via a small gate into a field. *A century and a half ago the sisters would have taken this route to the moors where they found such inspiration.* The part flagged path runs straight on to an old stile onto West Lane at the end of the village. Go left and immediately left again on Cemetery Road, with a pathway along the verge and rising onto the moorland slopes of Penistone Hill. *Immediately extensive views look over the Worth Valley, with Lower Laithe Reservoir just ahead.*

Just past a parking area opposite a cemetery take a broad, grassy path slanting down towards Lower Laithe Reservoir: off the moor it becomes enclosed above waterworks buildings to run a surfaced course out onto a road by the dam. *Stanbury sits on its little ridge across the water.* Turn briefly left uphill, then take a small gate on the right. Cross a field bottom beneath Intake Farm to a stile, then

WALK 16 • WORTH VALLEY

slant to a small gate at the top corner to join a walled green way. *This was the old way to Stanbury prior to construction of the reservoir.* Go briefly right, then take a gap by a gate on the left at a wood corner. A partly flagged path runs outside the trees, then part enclosed, emerging and tapering to a gap-stile into a field. Bear left across to a small gate overlooking steps down to a footbridge on a streamlet. Up the other side head away past a ruinous barn and along the left side of a crumbling wall to a barnyard: gates galore here as you approach and then leave by turning sharp left. An old way ascends the wallside to a stile onto Haworth Moor.

Turn right on a firm track past a ruin, narrowing into a broad path as the moor opens out. Just past the ruin leave by dropping to a ladder-stile in a wall recess just below. Bear left down the large sloping field to an old stile in the corner, overlooking the colourful valley floor. A little path drops left to South Dean Beck, doubling back a few strides to a footbridge across it. A few moist steps lead half-right to a wall-stile ahead, and then a thin path commences the re-ascent, slanting left a little up to an old wall. Resume uphill alongside a crumbled wall to a fence-stile, then easier going leads directly up towards a house at Cold Knoll on the skyline. A wall-stile puts you onto Back Lane just in front of it.

Turn briefly right (you could simply remain on this road), then take a path across a little grassy triangle to another access lane. Cross straight over this to a grassy walled way dropping away. *Ponden Reservoir is seen over to the left.* This descends onto an access track, where turn right to run a level course out onto a road. Go right to enter Stanbury at the point where the direct option comes in, and advance the length of the village. *Stanbury is a delightful street village spread along a distinct ridge between the Worth and Sladen Valleys. As well as the Friendly and Wuthering Heights pubs, here are St Gabriel's little church, a village school and the Manor House in amongst a range of attractive old cottages.*

Exiting the village on the now broader road, when the footway ends at the Oxenhope junction, continue down a couple of hundred yards further to a footpath signed along a slender walled snicket on the left. This runs grandly on, dropping down sharply right at the end into the hamlet of Lumb Foot. Continue down the road beneath the houses to the remains of an old mill on the left, and a farm bridge over the River Worth on the right just below. Advance a few strides further to cross instead on an attractive arched packhorse bridge on the modest 'river'. *Harnessed to supply numerous mills in times past, the Worth largely avoids human contact until it skirts the edge of Keighley to join the River Aire.*

Across the bridge a kissing-gate puts you back on the farm road, with two modern barns on the left. After them take a small gate in the fence on the right, and advance along the delightful pasture by the river. Squeezing through a tighter bank at the end, the river departs again but you pass through a gate in the fence corner just ahead, and advance along the base of the big sloping field with a fence on your right. At the end a gate/stile put you back on the riverbank, going briefly right to Long Bridge. *This is a delightful spot for a break, with herons and dippers in regular attendance. The shapely, stone-arched footbridge is a focal point of the Worth Valley's old packhorse routes. The narrow bridge hovers over a confluence of both the walk's streams, the River Worth and Sladen Beck, while beneath it is a ford.*

Cross the bridge and take the broad path rising away, with Sladen Beck down to your right. Through a stile the increasingly sunken way of Oldfield Lane winds up between forlorn walls to a ladder-stile into a garden at Lower Oldfield Farm. Turn left along the side of the house to a narrow walled snicket heading off at the end. This winds along to a tiny gate into a field. Advance along the top, then beyond an old field boundary cross to a stile opposite. Resume along anther field top, but part way along take a stile by a gate, and a broadly enclosed path runs on to emerge into a field. Advance along the bottom, becoming enclosed again to run on between graveyards beneath a Baptist Chapel. As a good path it ultimately emerges between houses onto North Street. For the church go right then left. Otherwise, go left past Lord Lane and fork next left down Mytholmes Lane.

After just 50 yards bear right down the near side of the terrace of South View. At the bottom a wall-gap puts you onto an enclosed path: go right to emerge into a recreational field. A tarmac path drops down the side to meet another one from the left, going right through a kissing-gate and along past white-walled Mill Hill Farm on the left. Drop down the track at the end, then swinging right to drop down a part surfaced, part cobbled way to emerge just above the footbridge at the station.

WALK 17

BROW MOOR

Beckside and moorland within a stone's throw of Haworth, enlivened by the sight, sound and smell of steam trains

START *Haworth (SE 034372; BD22 8NJ)*

DISTANCE *5¾ miles (9¼km)*

ORDNANCE SURVEY 1:25,000 MAP
Explorer OL21 - South Pennines

ACCESS *Start from the railway station. Car parks nearby. Bus and Worth Valley train from Keighley.*

Haworth station is home to the Keighley & Worth Valley Railway, a 5-mile branch from Keighley that closed to passengers in 1961. Enthusiasts rallied by later-to-be Keighley MP Bob Cryer rapidly formed a preservation society, and in 1968 the line triumphantly re-opened at the dawn of preserved steam railways. Though short in length it is one of the finest and friendliest lines, with stations at Keighley, Ingrow, Damems, Oakworth, Haworth and Oxenhope. It has been a location for numerous film and television projects, but the making of the classic family film 'The Railway Children' in 1970 earned the 'Worth Valley' lasting fame.

From the station forecourt cross the footbridge over the line, and turn left on Belle Isle Road. Passing a former cinema it joins Bridgehouse Lane at the end. Go left on the road bridge over the railway (with a view into the often busy yard) and turn right on

BROW MOOR • WALK 17

Brow Road at a war memorial. This immediately swings left to start climbing, but leave just as quickly by taking a few steps on the right. An enclosed path heads away, through a small gate and old kissing-gates along field bottoms as you shadow the long-drained course of a mill-cut. *Over to the right beyond modern industrial buildings, the railway runs parallel beyond Bridgehouse Beck.*

Before long the path bridges the old cut and runs on with it through trees, with Bridgehouse Beck below. At a kissing-gate at the cut's abrupt termination, the path forks. One branch drops to a footbridge on the beck, while yours runs straight ahead with a fence to the shell of a house. Ignore the track left and take a stile opposite: a part-flagged path gently rises with a wall to a small gate into a garden. Pass along the house front, and as the drive heads away, turn down a path to the right to rejoin the beck. Just a little further it reaches Donkey Bridge, a stone-arched packhorse bridge. *With the railway directly behind, this makes a nice spot to linger.*

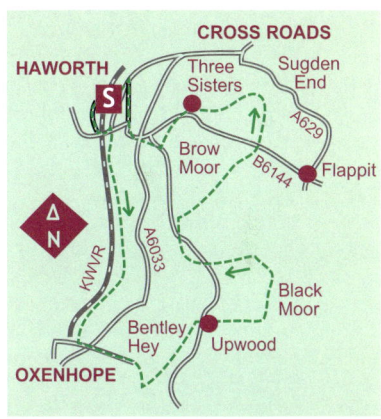

Don't cross but continue pleasantly upstream over a small sidestream and a kissing-gate to a stile accessing a footbridge on Bridgehouse Beck. The way resumes upstream to a solitary house and out on a drive, passing sewage works on the right. When the road bridges the beck, remain on the near side on a footpath sandwiched between beck and railway. At another footbridge re-cross the beck and the path runs along to emerge into a former mill yard at Wilton House, and out onto Harry Lane on the edge of Oxenhope. *The station is just down to the right (see WALK 18).*

Turn left up Harry Lane onto the A6033 Hebden Bridge road at the entrance to Manorlands. Cross straight over and up the steep Dark Lane, ignoring a branch right as it eases up and continuing up past a couple of houses to its demise into a rough track beyond

WALK 17 • BROW MOOR

Lower Croft House. Narrowing, it levels out to reach a renovated former farm at High Binns. *Big views look over Oxenhope village in its basin amid steep slopes rising to long moorland skylines.* Here leave the track by doubling back left on a short-lived walled green way to a stile onto the base of the heathery bank of Bentley Hey.

A path begins a steady ascent half-left, tracing the line of a sunken way through enthusiastic gorse and hawthorn. It gradually scales a tiny heather ridge before a longer, level section across more open country. *This provides lovely views over the valley, possibly with steam trains chugging away far below.* Approaching the end, the sunken way and gorse return to resume the slant uphill to a stile/gateway onto Black Moor Road. *On a clear day, look far to the north-west to see, above Oakworth Moor, the shapely outlines of Ingleborough and Penyghent, some 28 miles distant.*

Though a direct route goes left along this quiet road for three-quarters of a mile, a detour onto the edge of Black Moor adds an extra quarter-hour's interest. Almost at once turn right on Upwood Park caravan site access road. *From the walk's high point, massive views ahead feature Rombalds Moor, Almscliff Crag, Otley Chevin and Baildon Moor, while to the north are the Wharfedale heights of Great Whernside, Meugher and Simon's Seat.* Losing its surface, the lane expires at a bridle-gate onto heathery Black Moor. While the main path runs straight ahead, instead take a grassy wallside path declining very gently left to another broad track joining the moor. Pass through the gate onto this similar walled way. As Cuckoo Park Lane this nice sandy track gradually becomes a cart track and absorbs two driveways back out to rejoin Black Moor Road.

Turning right, Brow Moor wind turbine appears just ahead. For a brief escape from the road, within a minute take the grassy cart track of Upper Royd House Farm drive through open country on the left. As it turn sharply downhill, keep straight on a thin wallside path, before long rejoining the road. Within 100 yards a broad, stony path turns up the wallside onto a corner of Brow Moor. Unseen just yards to your left is the enormous Naylor Hill Quarry. The path improves considerably as it levels out and shadows the sturdy wall over the heathery brow and along to Brow Top Road (B6144). *Ahead are good views to Rombalds Moor and the Aire Valley beyond Keighley, also back over the upper reaches of the Worth Valley to Pendle Hill peeking over Watersheddles.*

BROW MOOR • WALK 17

Cross straight over and down the rough road of Hardgate Lane, which beyond Hardgate Cottage becomes no more than a pathway. Descending past old quarries, it becomes a rough road again at another house. Here take a stile on the left and a path crosses the field bottom to a stile at the end. Entering a heathery bank, a good path slants up above a small reservoir to a wall, then contours through bilberries to a sudden arrival at the Three Sisters Discovery Centre. *This was built as the Three Sisters pub, with no prizes for guessing the identity of the sisters.* Its drive leads left back up onto Brow Top Road, although the true path runs a parallel course through undergrowth on the left for the upper section.

Go right for just fifty paces to the Haworth/30mph signs. *Haworth itself returns to the scene, as does the ubiquitous wind turbine.* Here a good path heads off back across Brow Moor, angling very gently down back onto Black Moor Road just short of a house. Turn right just 30 paces then a path cuts a corner to drop through scrub back onto Brow Top Road. Just below is Hebden Road (A6033), beneath which the extremely steep Brow Road winds down through Haworth Brow into Haworth. Part way down at a sharp bend turn right on Victoria Road, through the heart of Haworth Brow's many stone terraces and passing the derelict Bronte Cinema before dropping down onto the B6142 at Mill Hey. Turn left to the station, just ahead.   *Flying Scotsman, Haworth*

WALK 18
NAB HILL

Bracing moorland tramping with magnificent views

START Oxenhope (SE 032353; BD22 9LB)

DISTANCE 6^1⁄$_2$ miles (10^1⁄$_2$km)

ORDNANCE SURVEY 1:25,000 MAP
Explorer OL21 - South Pennines

ACCESS Start from Mill Lane outside railway station. Parking on nearby Cross Lane. Bus and Worth Valley train from Keighley.

Oxenhope is a fine example of a Pennine mill community. The village sits in a basin with steep hills rising on three sides, through pastures to layers of moorland above. While illustrious neighbour Haworth draws the tourists, Oxenhope takes a back seat: recent changes have seen old mills replaced by housing. The squat church of St Mary the Virgin looks down from a lofty perch, witnessing, among other things, the annual straw race. This colourful pub crawl is a great charity fund-raiser, and incorporates the village centre Bay Horse among its more distantly ranged ports of call.

From the station entrance turn left along Mill Lane, quickly becoming Harry Lane to climb steeply to the A6033 Keighley-Hebden Bridge road. Cross and resume up the narrow and steep Dark Lane. At the first opportunity go right along the quiet back road of Yate Lane to emerge on Denholme Road in Lowertown. Go left a short way along the footway past a surviving mill chimney,

NAB HILL • WALK 18

then at the foot of a steep climb bear right on Jew Lane (beneath an overgrown burial ground). Avoid further, lesser forks right until a tiny grassy area at the handful of houses at Back Leeming. Again avoid the steep climb left, and bear right on a level cul-de-sac. Becoming a rougher access road it crosses a bridge to Egypt House. From a stile just above it, an enclosed path climbs left to a farm road at the corner of Leeming Reservoir. *Across the embankment of the 1877 dam, the scattered settlement of Leeming is dominated by its former mill, and has a pub, the cosy Lamb Inn.*

Ignore the embankment road, and bear right along a surfaced farm road to a fork, where go left to run between the fields. As it climbs away right, advance straight on an enclosed path just above the reservoir. This encounters a number of stiles before dropping to a kissing-gate and on to a footbridge on a side-stream near the reservoir head. As the path heads away from the bridge, ignore a branch right to a kissing-gate, and remain with the left one running alongside a tree-lined stream. Immediately after crossing it take a thinner path rising right alongside the stream. Through a gap-stile and small gate at the top it rises with a wall. This direct climb is maintained through several reedy but largely dry pastures to emerge at a substantial water conduit. The ladder-stile in front accesses a bridge over the conduit, then continue rising with an old wall. Higher up as the wall fades, the briefly fainter path swings left past a solitary tree to an old gateway. From here it rises left with a wall to meet a firm, level track at a three-way guidepost in front of a solid wall.

WALK 18 • NAB HILL

Turn right the short way to a gate/stile to begin the ascent of Hambleton Lane between old walls. *Almost at once you see the moor-top Thornton Moor Reservoir just to your left.* At a level section part way up, leave by a gate on the right, from where a rapidly improving sunken way slants across the moor to the grassy spoil heaps of old quarries. Merging with a path coming in from the left, bear right to commence a super level stroll. The cairn on Nab Hill beckons further along the moor edge as the grand path runs between these knolls and abandoned stones. *The tall turbines of Ovenden Moor windfarm loom large just across the flat moor-top, but more impressive are the massive views over Leeming, Oxenhope and much further beyond. The nine turbines of 2016 more than doubled the efficiency of the original 23 of 1993.*

Beyond the quarry site the path curves around the heads of Little Clough and Great Clough, divided by a moorland edge and more quarry remains. Just above the second clough, abandoned flags remain stacked alongside a stone pillar. A short stroll now rises imperceptibly past a circular shelter in a hollow to Nab Hill's waiting cairn. *Set amid further small-scale remains at an altitude of 1475ft/450m, the cairn is a fine specimen with a curved arm incorporating a shelter for the solitary rambler. This is a place to linger and savour extensive views. Westwards are the Lancashire heights of Boulsworth Hill and Pendle Hill, while beyond Bronte Country a massive panorama of Dales peaks includes Ingleborough, Penyghent, Fountains Fell, Buckden Pike and Great Whernside.*

From a more capacious stone shelter on the knoll just below, a thin path runs past a pile of stones to a cairn with extended arms on marginally higher ground. The little path curves around the slope to drop onto a broader quarry track just to the left. Virtually at the same time, Fly Flatts Reservoir (Warley Moor Reservoir on maps) appears ahead. The track curves down beneath old spoil heaps to run more moistly to a kissing-gate onto Nab Water Lane. Turn down this for a good hundred yards, and head off through a stile on the right. A faint path contours across the slope to a wall corner. Advance along the crumbled wall-top, noting that every wall in view is equally redundant. At the third descending wall a little path drops to bridle-gates enclosing a water conduit bridge, thence down to a bridle-gate back onto the road. Just a few paces left take a stile opposite, and a path sets off across the moor with

NAB HILL • WALK 18

an old wall. At a wall corner advance the short way to meet the conduit again. Turn right on its broad accompanying path to reach a gate onto the rough track of Far Peat Lane bridging the conduit.

Drop right the short way back onto the road, and turn left. Just beyond the bend under the prominent mast, as a steep descent is about to commence, take a stile on the left. Two field tops are crossed to join the rough Intake Lane. Rise left on this, briefly, before dropping to the Waggon & Horses pub on the A6033 Hebden Bridge road. Cross straight over and down a surfaced access road by colourful Hard Neze Clough, going right at the bottom to end at Hard Nese (Hard Naze on map). Keep straight on the continuing grassy way, emerging at the end onto the patch of moorland known as Stones. This locally popular heathery island is surrounded by green pastures. As the track goes sharp left, take the path rising to a wall corner to run very pleasantly along the crest.

At the end the path meets a track by a house, with an attractive footpath sign to the left. Go straight over and along an enclosed path past Olde Croft, with mullioned windows and a lovely garden. Through a small gate at the front the path runs out past another house and along its short drive to a junction with another drive. Leave at once however by advancing a couple of strides forward, and ignoring the flagged path ahead, take a gap-stile on the left. Descend a tiny enclosure and straight down a fieldside, with the church on your right. A little gate in the bottom corner sends an enclosed path down onto Shaw Lane on the edge of the village. Turn right to the junction with the main road. *The Bay Horse is just 100 yards further.* Take a broad, surfaced drive on the left, descending through the park to swing round to emerge onto Cross Lane. Turn down this to finish on Mill Lane.

Oxenhope from Stones

WALK 19 — BLACK MOOR

Immense variety linking woods, moors and an airy viaduct

START Cullingworth (SE 067367; BD13 5HD)

DISTANCE 6½ miles (10½km)

ORDNANCE SURVEY 1:25,000 MAP
Explorer OL21 - South Pennines

ACCESS Start from the village centre. Roadside parking. Bus from Keighley, Bradford, Bingley.

Cullingworth is a busy village largely spread along its main street, with the George and the Fleece pubs, a Post office and shops. The tall-spired church of St John the Evangelist overlooks attractive old cottages, and a converted Wesleyan Methodist chapel of 1824 sports a fine sundial. From the war memorial head south (away from the church) along the main street, and before the crossroads at the Fleece, turn right on cul-de-sac New School Lane. Passing the school, take the left-hand surfaced path at the end, beneath a Great Northern Railway Trail sign. *The village station stood to the right.* The path rises onto the old line, swinging left to immediately cross Cullingworth Viaduct. Through a gentle cutting between houses, it passes beneath a bridge to a junction with a farm road at a demolished bridge. You shall return here to finish.

For now, cross and resume on the tarmac path, rejoining the old line. Hewenden Reservoir appears on your right, and within a

BLACK MOOR • WALK 19

couple of minutes you emerge onto Hewenden Viaduct. *This 18-arched mighty landmark is an iconic feature of the old LNER line that climbed out of Keighley to Queensbury, where the celebrated Queensbury Triangle sent arms to Bradford and Halifax. Known as the Alpine Route for its succession of viaducts and tunnels through valleys and hills, the line succumbed to closure in 1955. Views look right over the reservoir and up to Denholme Edge, while left is a big view to the St Ives estate backed by Rombalds Moor.*

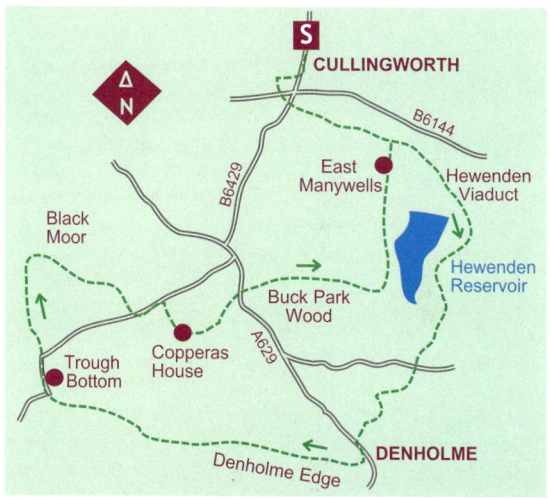

After a gate at the end the railway delves into an impenetrable tunnel. The tarmac path jinks right to rise to a bridle-gate onto the unsurfaced terminus of Station Road. *This is the site of Wilsden station, over a mile from the village.* Your way is right, through an iron kissing-gate and on a briefly enclosed green way into a field. With good reservoir and viaduct views the way runs left with the top wall before angling gently down to a kissing-gate beneath a house. A nice path runs on through trees, merging into the drive and quickly encountering the railway again at an overhead bridge.

Immediately before it, take a stile on the right and a path heads away parallel with the line above a tall embankment. At the end of this take a makeshift stile on the right: a few steps further

WALK 19 • BLACK MOOR

is a quarry access road. Go briefly left, meeting the old line but then taking an enclosed path on your right. Though local practice is to simply remain on the access road going left, the true path crosses a stile to emerge into a field. Advance along the side to a gate/stile back onto the road, with Whalley Lane a few strides further. Go a few paces left, and without passing under the rail arch, take a stile on the right. A path runs at mid-height along the embankment beneath the line, then soon briefly rises to be virtually alongside it. From a small gate on the right cross to an outer wall corner ahead, then rise with the wall on your left. At the top corner pass through a stile and go left along the field top, soon becoming briefly enclosed to join an access road. Turn right to rise to a gateway onto the A629 through Denholme. *The New Inn is just to your right.*

Turn left, passing an Independent Chapel of 1844 then cross to houses at Morningside. Head away along the short access road of Edge Bottom. As it ends, two grassy paths head away into the open country of Denholme Edge. Take the left one, ascending a sunken course through heather. Easing out at the top it runs on beneath a mast and high above modern housing. *Great Whernside is on the skyline far up the Dales, while Hewenden Reservoir and Viaduct are contrastingly close.* The path runs to a hand-gate in the wall ahead (not the corner stile). *Views ahead look to Black Moor over-topped by the Bronte moors: Ovenden Moor windfarm is over to your left. At some 1082ft/330m this is the walk's high point.*

A lovely green path resumes alongside the wall, and part way on, at a stile in it, bear right down a grassy path, slanting left down to a lone house. A concrete track is joined at a stile/gate behind it. Don't drop to its drive but go left through another gate, and a brief rise leads into a field edge. Here bear right on an inviting grass fenceside track. Passing through a gate ahead, a thinner grass path runs on through scattered trees to arrive above Booth House.

The path continues beyond the house to drop to a corner bridle-gate. Resume along a fenceside, soon revealing Bank House ahead and crossing straight to it on a grassy track. Pass through a gate into the yard and straight on to one back out. Ignore the driveway dropping away, and from a gate ahead cross to a ladder-stile. Now bear right down this extensive sloping pasture to find a corner gate/stile onto a bend of Trough Lane. Turn right a short way past the house at Trough Bottom to the next bend, where take a gate onto Black Moor. A good path rises away through heather to a brow: easily missed is a stone paved section just to the left. The path then drops gently to quickly meet a crumbling wall descending from the left. Pass through it on your left above the reedy hollow in front, and advance a few strides to meet another path crossing the wall and ditch in front.

Turn right over the ditch and immediately re-cross the wall. Double back right on a broad grassy path shadowing the reedy drain on your right. This level stroll leads to a junction with a grooved path coming in through heather from the left. Go straight on, after five minutes keeping right at a fork, and a grass track drops to a gate back onto Trough Lane opposite mullioned windowed Sand Beds Farm. Go briefly left and take the first right along a rough access road at Copperas House Farm. Immediately after the house on the right, take a kissing-gate on the left. A grassy wallside path heads away, and at the end another iron kissing-gate accesses an enclosed grassy way to reach Field Head Farm. Pass left and on through a private-looking gateway to pass left of another house and out on the drive back onto the A629.

Cross with care to a tiny gate left of a house, then descend a grass track towards the beginnings of the side valley of Milking Hole Beck. A continuing grass path drops down to bridge the stream beneath a small aqueduct just upstream. A glorious stroll ensues into Buck Park Wood in this deepening valley, passing beneath a line of massive gritstone boulders. Beyond a wall-stile, a tract of dense undergrowth leads out into the open: springtime bluebells add further colour. Here the path forks. The unofficial left branch keeps level to pick up the route across several pastures, but the right of way slants down to the right, through a lower wall-gap to run downstream with the beck.

A path junction is quickly reached at a bridge at the bottom. Don't cross but bear left, rising back up the field to a small gate in a wall at the top. A thin path heads away with a wall on the right, over which is Hewenden Reservoir backed by its viaduct. Dropping to a gate in a dip, a walled green way rises to a gate and on to join a farm track. Advance through another gate to the farming hamlet of East Manywells. After the first buildings advance to a bridle-gate ahead, and between further buildings follow the access road out to meet the old line again. Turn left to finish as you began.

WALK 20
HARDEN MOOR

A brilliantly colourful walk, featuring a superb waterfall and a memorable contrast of woodland and moorland

START Harden (SE 085383; BD16 1HS)

DISTANCE 5½ miles (8¾km)

ORDNANCE SURVEY 1:25,000 MAP
Explorer OL21 - South Pennines
Explorer 288 - Bradford & Huddersfield

ACCESS *Start from the village centre. Roadside parking, ideally on Wilsden road. Bus from Bingley.*

Harden is a sizeable village with strong links with Bingley, where its beck joins the Aire. Its once dominant mills are now replaced by housing. The Golden Fleece pub is centrally placed on the main road. Here also are a Post office, shops, St Saviour's church, a Congregational church and a former Wesleyan Reform Chapel of 1853, now two houses. From the mini roundabout turn along the Wilsden road to descend towards Harden Beck. After the houses on the right end, turn right along an enclosed access road leading to Ivy House Farm, with mullioned windows. *En route there is a good prospect of 17th century Harden Hall down to your left.* Passing along the front a faint path advances to a small corner gate ahead. Along the next fieldside another small gate puts you into scattered woodland, and the path runs pleasantly on through

HARDEN MOOR • WALK 20

bracken and springtime bluebells to quickly meet an access road. Bear left on this the short way to Goit Stock Cottages.

At a gate beyond the houses the cart track runs a little further to a fork. Your way is left, but first advance to the gate ahead to survey the intriguing chimney in the field here. *This is a lonely but iconic survivor from a former cotton mill, whose fumes arrived via a flue of which evidence also remains.* The enclosed onward path drops left onto an access road on the edge of a caravan park. Go left a few strides, then right at an information panel to shadow Harden Beck along to cross it by a footbridge putting you onto the end of another access road. *A century ago this area was known as Happy Valley, a hugely popular 1920s pleasure resort with various entertainment, including a café and ballroom in the old cotton mill, and a boating lake.* Turn right onto the start of a broad path into Goitstock Wood, with Harden Beck for company.

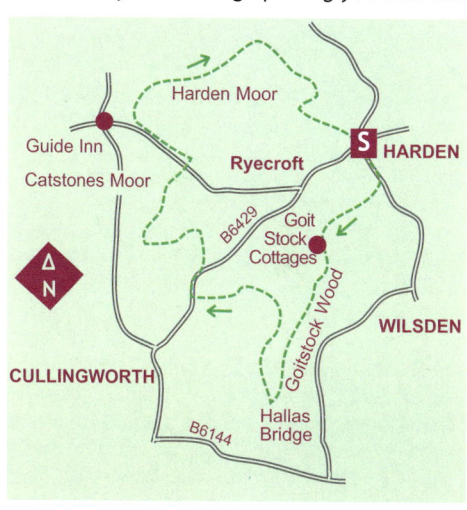

This lovely walk marches upstream through the trees of Goitstock Wood. *This is a hugely attractive section decorated by springtime bluebells: an early delight is the confluence of Cow House Beck with your main stream (now Hallas Beck) beneath a craggy knoll.* Gradually steeper slopes close in to reach Goit Stock Falls. *This is a beautiful drop over a craggy wall into a deep bowl, the centrepiece of these glorious woodlands.* A metal staircase makes light work of the little cliff before the delightful amble resumes past a smaller waterfall to soon reach a broad track at the modest Hallas Bridge.

WALK 20 • HARDEN MOOR

Cross the bridge and leave the track at once on a short path up to a stile on the brow. Rise right up an unkempt enclosure to a stile back into the woods, and a splendid level path heads away. Part way on is a fork: the right-hand option scales a gentle brow to run along the crest looking down on the outward valley to your right. The paths re-unite at a wall-stile at the far end, emerging into a large field surrounded on three sides by woodland. Head away down the centre to a footbridge on Cow House Beck.

Ascend the wallside behind, then turn sharp left to shadow a wall along the top of the large pasture above the beck. Part way on, a stile sends the route over the fence, only to shortly return at a crumbling wall corner at the start of Rough Plantation: local usage simply remains on the near side of this boundary. Passing through a gap in an old wall at the end of the trees, an improved path resumes with the wall along the top of two rough pastures all the way to a stile onto the B6429 Cullingworth-Harden road. *This is another enjoyable section above some colourful slopes, with Cullingworth church spire prominent.*

Cross to the footway and go right a short distance, then just beyond Cow House Farm turn left up Dolphin Lane. Engulfed in undergrowth, this slender bridle-path rises to a gate onto the open country of Catstones Moor. Follow a broad way left underneath a pocket wood until nearing a corner gate off the moor beneath a small stand of pines. Here take a path doubling back right through a kissing-gate to remain on the moor. Note that 100 yards before the corner a short-cut path slants up from a gap-stile in the fence, meeting the path that has come up from the corner. Undertaking a couple of sharp zigzags, the good path resumes by rising right through an old quarry site largely reclaimed by nature.

Beyond the long defunct quarries the splendid path rises more gently across the heathery moor, joined by a path from the right and levelling out. *Just after a tree you pass through a discernible section of Catstones Ring, an ancient trench and prominent mound rising left in a straight line.* The path runs on to a gate onto a road. *The direct route rises left for a short half-mile to the Guide Inn. This isolated landmark features a fading pictorial south-facing wall, and it appropriately presides over a hilltop junction of ways. Easily missed opposite the pub stands an inscribed stone guide-post, pointing the way to Bingley, Haworth, Keighley and Halifax.*

HARDEN MOOR • WALK 20

A road-free option crosses straight over to a wall-stile, from where a thin path rises left through heather alongside a fence guarding an immense working quarry. As the fence turns off on the brow, advance through a little scrub onto a broad, firm path. Go left the few strides to reach a kissing-gate back onto the road, and shadow it along through parking verges towards the Guide Inn in view ahead. At a small parking verge a little beyond the main, extended one, take a kissing-gate back onto the moor. A broad, firm path heads directly away, swinging left around a fenced, quarry hollow to reach a junction at the end of the fence. With Harden Moor outspread ahead, simply remain on this broad, main path in a direct march across the heart of the moor. At the second cross-paths note the splendid stone flagged quarrymans' track going left.

Keep straight on to quickly arrive at a gritstone cluster on a knoll. As the main path swings right here, instead take the path dropping right from the boulders through bracken to a kissing-gate onto a broad path by the moor edge wall. Go right and then follow it around the corner, descending steadily to soon reach the head of wooded Deep Cliff Hole. At the path's lowest point – on a walled embankment marked by a stile in the wall - fork right on a thinner, level path to a small gate in a fence. After a very slight rise this runs a splendid level course through scattered trees between the moor and the steep wooded drop of the clough. Avoiding any lesser forks it runs towards a wall, bearing right to reach the wall corner at a path junction. With the wall to your left, the path drops down to leave the trees at a wall-stile.

The path slants down a small field to a hidden stile and stone steps onto an access road. Turn right, past a couple of houses and in around the wooded environs of Deep Cliff Hole again. As it turns to climb steeply through private gates, take a gate/stile on the left from where a path crosses a field to a gap-stile in front of the Coach House (Spring Farm). The path neatly skirts the garden and resumes to Spring House, just ahead. Immediately before it an iron gate sends a narrow, enclosed footpath down to the left. This soon accompanies the beck downstream, passing modern housing on the site of a mill. Entering suburbia, advance straight on to join the main road in the village centre, emerging rather handily alongside the pub.

WALK 21
ROMBALDS MOOR

Bracing moorland strides sandwiched by a lovely valley

START East Morton (SE 099419; BD20 5SP)

DISTANCE 8½ miles (13½km)

ORDNANCE SURVEY 1:25,000 MAP
Explorer 297 - Lower Wharfedale & Washburn Valley

ACCESS Start from the village centre. Roadside parking. Bus from Keighley and Bingley.

East Morton boasts the Busfeild Arms pub and some attractive old corners, along with St Luke's church and a Bethel Chapel of 1845. From the pub head east on the main road, swinging up to a junction with Green End Road. Turn left, passing Manor Farm on the left. Leaving the terraces behind, a fork is reached in front of the grounds of Morton Hall. Take the rough road (Upwood Lane) left, and at a junction below a farm go right, a good track rising gently through pleasant surrounds to a gate into Sunnydale. As it swings to cross the beck at a colourful guidepost, advance to the dam of Sunnydale Reservoir, a tranquil, wooded scene.

Across the dam the path climbs wooden steps to a junction. Turn left, soon transforming into a superb woodland path, quickly rising to a small dam on a shelf, with Glen Farm beyond. Through an old wall the path runs faithfully on the wood top, crossing a footbridge to reach a corner where another bridge is crossed beneath a waterfall on Sweet Well Dike. The path doubles back left, then right through another old wall to remain on the wood top, a super stroll to reach a gate at the end. Joining a cart track, drop left over Bradup Beck and rise through a gate to shadow a wall towards Upwood Hall. *Over to the right is a big sweep of Morton Moor.* Before the farm buildings the track turns sharp right to rise away, becoming enclosed to meet Ilkley Road. *Upwood was home to the Busfield family whose arms adorn the village pub.*

Turn right, dropping to cross Bradup Beck then climbing up onto Rombalds Moor, passing a well at a stone trough dated 1853. At the top of the pull useful verges lead along to the road summit at Keighley Gate (Whetstone Gate on maps). Pass through the gate and leave the now unsurfaced road by turning right up a fence-side path past a small mast. As the wall becomes

solid your path becomes stone flagged, and a near level stroll leads quickly to the Thimble Stones. *A brace of boulders stand amid a host of smaller rocks, the majority being found over the wall.*

The flagged path diverges from the wall here, angling across to the OS column at 1319ft/402m on the summit of Rombalds Moor. En route, a few small boulders feature the Puddle Stone. *This 2012 addition to the landscape features the work of poet Simon Armitage, part of his South Pennine Stanza Stones series. The*

WALK 21 • ROMBALDS MOOR

extensive view from the moor's summit offers a host of features across the valley, from Buckden Pike and Great Whernside down to Simon's Seat, Beamsley Beacon, Menwith Hill and Almscliff Crag.

Resume on the continuing flagged path, declining at a gentle angle towards Wharfedale before leveling out atop a minor edge at White Crag Moss. A few minutes along here you reach a crossroads with a regular path, marked by a cairn. Turn right, rising gently to the brow and quickly reaching the ridge-wall at Ashlar Chair. *This massive boulder marks the meeting point of Bingley, Morton, Ilkley and Burley Moors.* Through the hand-gate you commence a return to the valley, a clear but initially moist path heading down Bingley Moor with the old wall. Suddenly a narrow flagged section begins, and though intermittent it does an excellent job. Before long this takes you away from the wall, angling across the moor and dropping gently down. After the last of the flags this steady slant ultimately bridges a drain and broadens for the last few strides to meet a fine track. Turn left for a contrastingly effortless stride to a gate alongside a lone house to meet Otley Road at Drake Hill.

Cross over and along Heights Lane just as far as a stile on the right. A faint path descends slightly left to a moist area preceding a fence-stile. Just ahead is another stile on the right, and then a reedy corner with two plank bridges leads to another wall-stile. Now head down a contrastingly dry pasture to find a stile slightly left. From this stile cross a few reeds and a streamlet and head away down a quite slender pasture, initially with the right-hand wall then bearing left into the centre as a modest grassy path descends through colourful terrain. On approaching the concrete drive of Hill Top Lane with a house on your left, turn right down it the short way to a gate onto Carr Lane at the top of Micklethwaite.

Turn left into Micklethwaite and descend the sloping green to a narrow bend at attractive High Fold. Turn right down Beck Road before the Methodist chapel. Remain on this access road as it swings left through a communal yard, then right to the last house. Just ahead is a fork as Holroyd Mill access road drops left: go straight ahead along an inviting enclosed path down to Hebble Bridge, a high footbridge on Morton Beck. Across, the path turns right, briefly upstream before bearing left up a flight of steps onto an access road, Cliffe Mill Fold. Rise briefly left and keep straight on, becoming Dimples Lane to emerge back into the centre.

RIVERBANK & TOWPATH

WALK 22

Very easy walking alongside the valley's two waterways

START Bingley (SE 105394; BD16 2RH)

DISTANCE 6 miles (9½km)

ORDNANCE SURVEY 1:25,000 MAP
Explorer 288 - Bradford & Huddersfield

ACCESS Start from the parish church on main road. Central car parks. Bus and train from Keighley, Bradford and Leeds.

Bingley is a bustling former industrial town which has happily retained some older corners, notably the environs of All Saints church. In Myrtle Park is the Georgian Town Hall (formerly the Ferrand family's Myrtle Grove), while nearby is the Market Hall, complete with market cross and stocks. Bingley Show and Bingley Music Live are prestigious annual events that take place in the park. A remarkable aspect of the town is that the River Aire flowing parallel to its busy main street has repelled any development on its western bank, while another odd feature is the 2003 by-pass which steers an ingenious course through, not around, the town.

From the setted Old Main Street by the parish church, take the B6429 Harden road (Millgate) to Ireland Bridge on the River Aire. *This links the historic Old White Horse with the Brown Cow in a location that has suffered numerous floods, notably in December 2015 when both pubs and several houses were damaged.* Before

WALK 22 • RIVERBANK & TOWPATH

the bridge take an enclosed path on the left between buildings, within a minute passing Ailsa Well. *This is identified by a sign on a wall: just through a gap in the wall and across a track, stone steps descend to a stone trough with water tinkling in.*

The path runs on through the riverbank's greenery to emerge into Myrtle Park, and advance the short way further to a large iron footbridge on the Aire. Across, head directly away the few paces to a path rising into woodland. Up a few steps is a junction: go left, and when another branch climbs steps to the right, keep straight on your path rising gradually the short way to the wood top. It runs along to soon emerge via a gap-stile at a solitary house. Pass along the front and on a faint path through the field ahead, with the river just below. Narrowing between trees, just a few steps further you find Harden Beck has replaced the river on your left, and just ahead is a gap-stile accessing Beckfoot Bridge. *Beck Foot is an idyllic location, with 18th century arched bridge, ford and desirable cottages.*

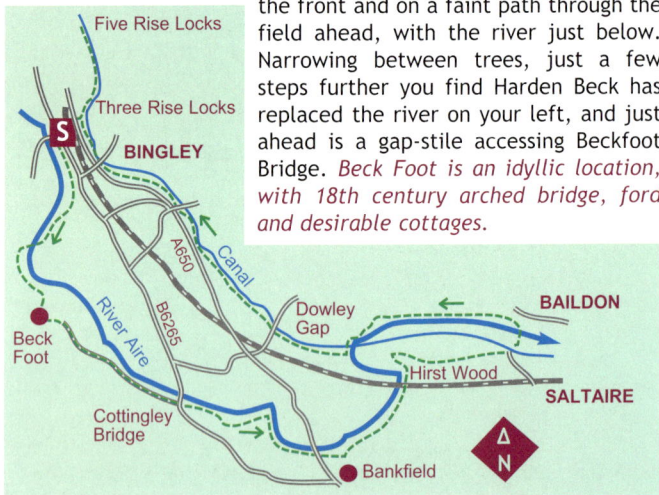

Cross the bridge and head away along peaceful Beckfoot Lane, out of sight of the river in greenery, on between sports fields and Shipley golf club where suburbia is reached. The river returns and the footway leads along to the B6265 at Cottingley Bridge. Cross the road to a stile in the wall opposite, and a steep flight of steps drop you on the riverbank. Across a garden edge the riverbank path heads downstream by garden fences before emerging into sports fields. Simply remain with the river, a spell in scrub after passing a bridge sees further sports fields before entering denser scrub at

RIVERBANK & TOWPATH • WALK 22

the end. The path passes beneath the by-pass bridge and on into further trees. Through a wall-gap the path enjoys a tall-walled snicket section outside the grounds of Bankfield, a large house long used as a hotel. As the snicket turns right at the end, your hedged path continues straight on the riverbank. *During this lovely section I witnessed a pair of kingfishers in action.*

At the far end another snicket goes off, while your path bridges a sidestream to enter Hirst Wood beneath a corner of Nab Wood Cemetery. Passing beneath a railway bridge, the path heads downstream through trees, and before long rises slightly from the river when a thinner branch stays with it. On the brow a junction is reached: turn right, curving briefly uphill then left (ignoring a lesser one to the right) to run a straight, level course through Hirst Wood. At the end the path emerges into a car park at the Leeds-Liverpool Canal. Turn left on the bridge over the canal at Hirst Lock. *Saltaire is just minutes further along the towpath (see WALK 25).*

Turn a few steps right to the lock, then at a gap in the wall on the left a path drops onto an access track. Past this cross a metal footbridge on the Aire. With housing in front, go immediately left on the grass to a footbridge on a sidestream. Now go left the few strides to a riverbank rowing club. *Opposite across the old weir is Hirst Mill.* A footpath resumes upstream, a lovely stroll as fields are replaced by trees. This runs grandly on the bank to rise at the end onto the canal towpath at the end of an aqueduct over the Aire.

Turn right the short way to cross Bridge 206, and the towpath resumes on the other side, passing Dowley Gap Locks and beneath a road bridge on Wagon Lane at the Fisherman's Inn. The path resumes through greenery to the edge of Bingley. Squeezed by the by-pass it runs opposite old mills and housing, then parallel with the by-pass to arrive opposite Damart Mill, and the Three Rise Locks. To the left is the footbridge by which you will finish, but first advance five minutes further along the towpath to the iconic Five Rise Locks, showpiece of the Leeds-Liverpool Canal. *Here, for over 200 years, five interlinking locks have lifted boats up a watery staircase - a fascinating spectacle and a fine piece of engineering. At the top stands a popular café.* Retrace steps to the Three Rise Locks and cross the high footbridge (a modern replacement for the evocatively named Treacle Cock Alley) over road and railway, dropping down to finish at the junction by the church.

WALK 23
ST IVES & DRUID'S ALTAR

A wealth of interesting features amid wooded landscapes

START *Bingley (SE 105394; BD16 2RH)*

DISTANCE *6½ miles (10½km)*

ORDNANCE SURVEY 1:25,000 MAP
Explorer 288 - Bradford & Huddersfield

ACCESS *Start from the parish church on main road. Central car parks. Bus and train from Keighley, Bradford and Leeds.*

For a note on Bingley, see page 81. From the setted Old Main Street by the church, take the B6429 Harden road (Millgate) over Ireland Bridge on the River Aire. *This links the historic Old White Horse with the Brown Cow in a location that has suffered from numerous floods, notably in December 2015 when both pubs and several houses were damaged.* Before the bridge end, a gap on the right sends a snicket between houses. *Just past this point note the Benjamin Ferrand stone of 1713 set into the wall.* Emerging onto a back street, turn right as an unsurfaced road heads upstream with the river through increasingly wooded surrounds. This access road later leaves the river to run beneath wooded slopes to Raven Royd. *This lovely old house features arch-headed mullioned windows, and fronts a characterful farmyard scene.* Pass to its right, on through the yard, and straight on the continuing enclosed access track through an equestrian landscape to Cophurst.

ST IVES & DRUID'S ALTAR • WALK 23

Pass left of the house out into a field. A cart track continues on beneath a wooded bank, and up behind the grassy knoll of Hutler Hill to a small pasture, with another path coming in from the left. Advance to a gate/stile in front, and a grassy track runs on a tapering enclosure to a stile onto an access road at the scattered hamlet of Marley. *Just over to the right is another fine building, Marley Hall.* Go left the few yards towards Blakey Cottage with its 1694 datestone, but remain on the rough road climbing steeply left. Approaching the house of Marley Brow above, bear right on the continuing track. This slants up increasingly colourful pasture towards the lone house at Transfield Hole.

A delightful green track now continues above the house, slanting up the colourful surrounds of Marley Brow. *This stage enjoys extensive views over the Aire Valley. While the elevated Rombalds Moor skyline might be fairly timeless, the lower ground is dominated by a dual carriageway, a housing development and a golf course.*

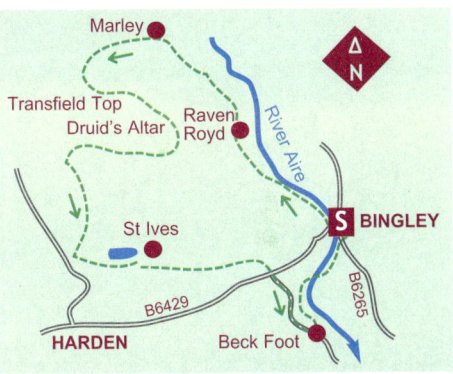

Swinging left, the track rises to end at a gate/kissing-gate in a wall. Through this a good path climbs for some time up a bracken-cloaked enclosure. Higher up it bears right towards the top corner. Just short of the top, as the path thins, take a left fork slanting up a groove to merge with a level path along the top. With a wall just above, turn left on this delightful path through the largely still bracken-draped Transfield Top. Soon entering more trees you ultimately emerge onto an access road. Cross straight over and along the short way through increasingly open heathery surrounds to the Druid's Altar. *Here sizeable gritstone outcrops form a well-defined edge in colourful open country, the finest location from which to survey the aforementioned view. If the Druids did offer sacrifices here, they certainly chose a grand spot!*

WALK 23 • ST IVES & DRUID'S ALTAR

At the early and abrupt end of the rocks leave the edge on a path bearing right to run through bracken and scattered trees the short distance to meet Altar Lane at its junction with the access road you very recently crossed. Straight across take the gateway into St Ives estate. *The country estate of St Ives was once owned by the Knights Templar and Knights Hospitallers, and later by the monks of Rievaulx Abbey. The estate passed to the Ferrand family in 1636, and into public ownership in 1928. Some 400 acres cover much of this hillside between Harden and Bingley. Within its high walls are a fine mix of woodland, moorland and farmland, along with a 19th century mansion, golf course and sports turf research centre.*

At once leave the main bridleway by turning right through a kissing-gate onto a firm path. This rises ever gently, alongside a pasture then into a belt of trees, remaining near the boundary wall until confronted by a lesser wall alongside a kissing-gate off Altar Lane. *This offers massive views up the Aire Valley.* Here the path turns sharp left to begin a long, steady, straight descent by the upper part of a golf course. Initially dark and enclosed, it improves to run alongside aptly-named Heather Park. On re-entering trees the path drops down to Lady Blantyre's Rock. *The eponymous woman came to sojourn at this large gritstone boulder, and after her death in 1875 her son-in-law William Ferrand placed an inscribed tablet here. Being something of a dignitary himself, the Ferrand Monument was erected after his death in 1889, and is located just fifty yards up behind the rock.*

Below Lady Blantyre's Rock the broad path delves into deeper woodland before swinging left, with the main path soon running alongside Coppice Pond. This extensive haven for birdlife leads you onto the access road through the estate: a café stands just to the left. Cross straight over to a broad path slanting back into trees. Passing through a gateway in a wall this runs on beneath a grassed area and then below the mansion itself. Remain on this broad path running a largely level course, then dropping slightly to meet

ST IVES & DRUID'S ALTAR • WALK 23

the estate road again. Bear right with it, using a parallel path to its left to arrive at a lodge. Beyond it another parallel path drops down into a car park just below. Rejoin the road for a few yards, but as it winds down towards the B6429 Harden-Bingley road, bear left on a broad path back into trees. This immediately forks: take the right branch, descending to a wall-gap onto the road.

Cross with care and escape down peaceful Beckfoot Lane. At the bottom it loses its surface as it runs past a converted mill to reach Beck Foot. *This location features an 18th century arched bridge, a ford and desirable cottages.* Don't cross the bridge but take a stile on the left just before it, and head away through the field. A modest brow reveals the Aire just below, and Myrtle Park opposite. Rising to pass along the front of a solitary house, advance to a stile into trees. The path runs on a short while before slanting down to a fork, where drop right into a large open space just across which is a substantial iron bridge on the Aire. *Commemorating the Festival of Britain in 1951, it gives access to Myrtle Park.*

Cross the bridge and for the town centre go straight up through the park. For the church turn left on the riverside walk, a pleasant stroll clinging to the wooded bank all the way along to emerge alongside Ireland Bridge. Towards the end is Ailsa Well, identified by a sign on a wall. *Just through a wall-gap and across a track, stone steps descend to a stone trough with water tinkling in.*

Opposite: Beckfoot Bridge *At the Druid's Altar*

WALK 24
BAILDON MOOR

Historic paths explore moorland, pasture and valley

START *Baildon (SE 154397; BD17 6LX)*

DISTANCE *7¼ miles (11½km)*

ORDNANCE SURVEY 1:25,000 MAP
Explorer 288 - Bradford & Huddersfield
Explorer 297 - Lower Wharfedale & Washburn Valley

ACCESS *Start from market cross in Towngate in village centre. Car park. Bus from Shipley and Bradford, rail station one mile.*

Baildon was an important market site in centuries past, with packhorse routes radiating in all directions. The market cross is of medieval origin, with adjacent stocks: close by is the Frances Ferrand memorial fountain. From the roundabout turn up Hallcliffe past the Ian Clough Hall. *This recalls a Baildon climber killed on Annapurna in 1970.* Pass St John's church to a junction, and go left on Heygate Lane. At a junction at the end keep on a sports club drive, and a surfaced path continues on between sports fields. Briefly enclosed, it runs on to emerge onto a corner of Baildon Moor.

Just in front, a lane known as Moorside drops to an equestrian centre. *Miners' and quarrymens' cottages existed here until the 1960s. Ahead is a lovely prospect over the valley you are about to cross to Hawksworth.* Just short of the buildings a thin path drops right back onto the access road, then a briefly enclosed path drops

BAILDON MOOR • WALK 24

down by a paddock. Through another small gate, a stile at the bottom puts you into a field. Continue down fieldsides, crossing to the other side at a hand-gate to descend to a leafy glade and over a grassy brow into the sylvan charms of Hawksworth Spring. Advance on the slender clearing and the path descends a wooded bank to Gill Beck.

Crossing the small beck on stepping-stones, opt for the footpath slanting right and ascending through trees to a wall-stile into a field. Continue rising and soon the path transfers to the other side by a stile and slab bridge to a corner of a golf course.

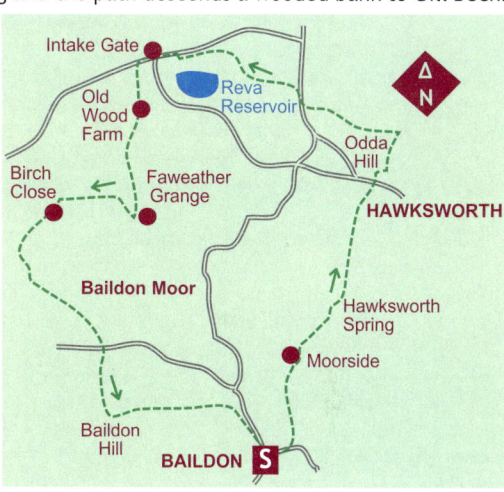

The path ascends the side through undergrowth, leaving via a corner stile to resume ascending meadow sides. A final pair of stiles leads across a yard to a narrow way between houses onto the road through Hawksworth. *Hawksworth is a house-proud village clinging to a busy minor road. Looking as rural as Arncliffe or Linton, it sits just outside the suburban limits of Guiseley. To the right are delightful gritstone cottages with manicured lawns and roses round the doors, while at the far end is Hawksworth Hall.*

Opposite, a snicket winds up behind a house to rise alongside Hawksworth Wood. *Part way up, a permissive path turning right into the trees makes a very brief variant, especially worthwhile at bluebell time. Heading away and swinging left, within a couple of minutes you reach an angled cross-paths. Here double back left to rise to rejoin the public path at the wood corner.* Here a kissing-gate puts you onto Odda Hill, where a faint path advances to the brow of the field to view an extensive Wharfedale panorama. Just

WALK 24 • BAILDON MOOR

a little further you look down on a colourful gorse bank. *Below is Menston beneath the hinterland of Otley Chevin; to the right Guiseley; Otley sits in the Chevin's shadow. Across the Wharfe the vast moors of Denton and Askwith fill the northern skyline.*

Fence-stiles lead in and out of the gorse, then the path descends the bank to a farm track at the bottom. Turn left, initially rough beneath the gorse bank but beyond a stile/gate it improves to run a grassy course to a stile/gate onto Hillings Lane opposite Moor View House. Go very briefly right to a stile opposite, and head away to the end of a surfaced drive. From a stile on the right trace the wall rising away to be ushered right to a pair of stiles onto the foot of a corner of open country. A good path rises away, passing left of the gorse-draped knoll ahead, with Reva Reservoir below. From a gate/kissing-gate the access road to its sailing centre leads out to busy Bingley Road. *Ahead is the extensive Hawksworth Moor.* However, an unmapped permissive path avoids the initial dodgy section of road: without joining the road take a kissing-gate on the left, and an enclosed path runs parallel with the road to another such gate onto it. Here a verge path runs the two minutes left to a junction at Intake Gate. *This was once an inn of dubious clientele known as the Gaping Goose.* Cross the side road then advance just a short way further to take the drive on the left to Old Wood Farm.

Pass right of the buildings, and as the access road swings left behind them, instead take a gate in front. An old way heads off along the fieldside ahead, encountering stone flags on this historic packhorse route of Old Wood Lane. Beyond a gate it becomes enclosed, dropping down and swinging right for a delightful stroll between old walls, then dropping down again to join a track. Turn right on this to re-cross Gill Beck at a ford and splendid clapper bridge. Through a gate the enclosed track rises away, absorbing a driveway then quickly arriving at a junction of historic ways: just 100 yards to the left is Faweather Grange. *This was a small grange of Rievaulx Abbey: the monks mined ironstone nearby, while a stone mine opened as recently as 1889 was worked to a depth of 90 feet for flags and roofing stone.*

From the junction your onward route is the enclosed track right, between houses then rising to an open tract. As it becomes surfaced and rises right, go straight on along the back of Birch Close Farm. Just past it a gate puts you onto a short-lived, walled grassy

BAILDON MOOR • WALK 24

track, Birch Close Lane. At the end a sandy equestrian track comes in from the right, but your path crosses it to run a parallel field bottom course. At the end another sandy track comes in from the right, and the main one curves back round left: another goes straight ahead - cross and go straight ahead, now alongside one on your left. This quickly meets another, with a gate ahead onto Baildon Moor.

Baildon Moor is shared with many other leisure users, though prime concern is an awareness of golf balls. A firm bridle-path heads away, but after 50 yards, past a tee, bear left up a rougher path and rise very gently alongside a fairway. Part way on, cross this and take a clear path slanting steeply up onto Pennythorn Hill to a green on your left. Merging with another path from the left, continue rising with a fairway on your left. On the very brow of Pennythorn Hill, with the Eldwick-Baildon road close by, pass another green to join the road at a parking area on its brow.

Cross the road, and with Dobrudden Farm road bearing off left, instead ascend a grassy path, rising to a brow to reveal the moor-top Ordnance Survey column. On meeting Dobrudden farm road, go very briefly right along it to reach a curious tor-like feature. *The moor was mined for coal from at least 1387, and later for steam engines for mills: the last pit closed about a century ago. What we have here are slagheaps - locally the 'cinder caves'.* Now leave the farm road to rise left the two minutes to the summit of the walk, the OS column at 925ft/282m on Baildon Hill. *Also featuring two benches and a topograph, its panorama reaches to distant power stations beyond Bradford, and along the Pennine crest to Keighley. Bingley Moor represents the all-embracing Rombalds Moor. Baildon Moor was purchased by Bradford Corporation for £7000 in 1897, and in the 1920s was the scene of illegal gambling rings.*

Resuming the eastward direction a broad path (one of many) crosses the plateau, running left of some hummocks alongside a sizeable pool. Crossing a grassy track at right-angles, your path now descends more, over another cross-path and straight down a bracken bank to the near wall corner. It remains on the moor between a fairway and housing, with much flagging underfoot. At the foot of the moor take a firm path branching right, absorbing another and down through a kissing-gate to approach the golf club-house. Before its drive the way bears left over a rough parking area onto the road off the moor, and turn right to finish.

WALK 25 SHIPLEY GLEN

An iconic landmark on the edge of a World Heritage Site

START *Saltaire (SE 139380; BD18 3LQ)*

DISTANCE *6¼ miles (10km)*

ORDNANCE SURVEY 1:25,000 MAP
Explorer 288 - Bradford & Huddersfield

ACCESS *Start from railway station. Roadside parking, car park.*

Saltaire was a mill village created by Sir Titus Salt, who moved his workers to this green-field site from the polluted air and slums of Bradford. From 1850 hundreds of terraced stone dwellings were built to house the workforce of his new worsted processing mill. This outstanding piece of industrial architecture, 550ft long and 6 storeys high, is a sight to behold. The village's grid-iron system remains, along with schools, almshouses, hospital and institute that followed. Most buildings function as originally intended, and Saltaire was designated a World Heritage Site in 2001.

From the railway station turn down Victoria Road. *Note, in spacious grounds, the finest of Salt's buildings: the Congregational Church (now the United Reformed Church) was built in 1859 in rich Italian style, with a semicircular front and ornate circular tower.* The road crosses the Leeds-Liverpool Canal to the Boathouse pub on the Aire. A footbridge gives access to Roberts Park, a tribute to Salt's work and important amenity for his workers. Head away from

SHIPLEY GLEN • WALK 25

the bridge through the edge of the park onto Higher Coach Road. Bearing left along it, a path strikes across playing fields to Shipley Glen Tramway. *'Gateway to the Moors', Shipley Glen Cable Tramway was built in 1895, and its open cars haul visitors up the wooded bank to the glen.* To its left a surfaced path climbs through trees to the top station where go left on Prod Lane, passing the old funfair site. A little further along is the Old Glen House pub with tearoom, directly behind which is the open country of the glen.

Now strike out across grassy terrain, the best line being atop a fine gritstone edge that forms above the wooded bank. This avoids traffic if not people, and it serves the route well throughout the length of the glen. *A brief diversion takes in Bracken Hall, now a countryside centre with exhibitions and displays on local history and wildlife. The glen has been a place of popular resort since people first escaped city grime for weekend fresh air. Known as Brackenhall Green until the romanticised 'glen' was appended in the 1840s, its proximity to the vast Bradford metropolis ensures a regular stream of visitors. The depths of the glen are rich in natural woodland, though most folk tend to perambulate along the spacious green.*

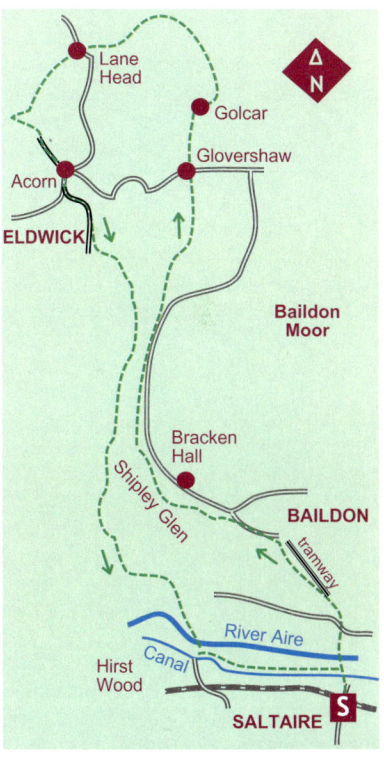

Only 100 yards past the hall is the Soldiers' Trench, a Bronze Age circle up to 50 yards across. Though part destroyed by the road, a double circle of at least 60 stones can still be seen.

WALK 25 • SHIPLEY GLEN

The path now runs above more substantial rocks, decorated in dry spells by the chalk of climbers. *Set back up to the right is Baildon Moor.* Towards the end the road squeezes in again, and only a minute after the attendant wall turns up the moor, a parting of the ways is reached: as the road bears right, ignore a broad path dropping left to the wooded upper confines of the glen. Instead, advance along the broad grassy way directly ahead, traversing level ground as it enters bracken. Passing above a quarry site reclaimed by heather, a broader track is crossed and your now thinner path runs the short way further to the trees ahead. At the edge of the moor a tiny footbridge leads to a wall-stile and a smashing path shadowing Glovershaw Beck upstream.

A nice waterfall is passed, and approaching a minor confluence an inscribed boundary stone stands by the path. The path runs on beneath barns at Glovershaw, staying with the beck to emerge via a stile onto Glovershaw Lane. *Fading paint on the farm proclaiming 'TEAS' recalls the days when refreshment might be found at such wayside farms.* Cross over and up the drive opposite to its terminus at Golcar Farm. *Astride a crossroads of old ways, this approach is on the line of a monastic route linking a grange at Bingley with Faweather, a smaller grange visited in WALK 24.*

Don't turn into the yard but advance a few steps further to a bridle-gate at the end of the buildings: ignore the continuing grassy way ahead. Head away between equestrian paddocks, and then a continuing green way rises between fields, emerging via a bridle-gate at the top to run a still enclosed course left with a wall to a gate/stile. Maintain the line across a field, rising steadily towards a wall-corner. Don't advance to the corner gate set back, but turn left at the outer wall corner on a thin path. This same course is maintained through a gate and winds around a field edge, at the end becoming enclosed to run a pleasant grassy course out to a gate/gap onto Otley Road at Lane Head.

Go left a few paces and turn right into the yard of exclusive housing. With an attractive cottage on the right advance briefly on, quickly forking right a few paces to be faced with a house in front. Bear right here on a briefly enclosed path emerging into a parking area for further houses. *Across the yard is Eldwick Hall, a splendid old house with a 1696 datestone and mullioned windows.* Your way is immediately left on an enclosed path between gardens down to

SHIPLEY GLEN • WALK 25

a small gate into an unkempt enclosure. The path drops to a small gate onto a track. A couple of paces left the path resumes down this next pasture to a corner gate/stile at the bottom. A much improved continuation descends the wallside, and part way down takes a stile into the start of a small wood. The path runs down the side to emerge over a grassy bridge onto an access road with the Old Corn Mill on your right. Go left, and remain on this surfaced lane as it winds out past another house and drops alongside wooded Eldwick Beck to emerge at The Green on the edge of Eldwick. Passing the Acorn Inn you rejoin Otley Road. *Along to the right is another pub, The Birches, and a Post office/shop.*

Turn right and ascend the roadside footway beneath a former chapel of 1888. On the brow cross and head off left along Saltaire Road. Passing exclusive housing it runs above tree-lined Loadpit Beck to reach the start of Shipley Glen after the last house. As it forks ignore Lode Pit Lane going right, and descend the rough road to a stone-arched bridge on the beck: the edge of Shipley Glen is immediately over the bridge. Don't cross, however, as your way takes a good path into the trees on the right, rising slightly before running on to quickly meet another path coming down from Lode Pit Lane. Resume along this, through the trees with the wooded beck below. This remains your course for a good while, always with a boundary containing gardens just to your right.

Ultimately the sturdy wall turns sharp right at the end, with the woods opening out. The path goes with it to enter an old walled track. Turn left down this, with an intriguing stone floor. Quickly dropping to a fork, bear right through an extravagant, 7ft tall iron gate, and an enclosed path drops to the bottom, where its swings right as a broader track to South Lodge. *This was the entrance to the grandiose mansion of Milner Field, completed in 1869 for Sir Titus Salt's son. Its history is littered with tragedy, and immense running costs saw it demolished in the 1950s.* Keep left along the broadening rough road, dropping very gently to arrive at an access road going right immediately before a bridge and modern housing. This runs the short way towards the river opposite Hirst Mill. Just before, go left on a footbridge over the beck, and a path runs along a grassy sward past modern housing. Quickly reaching a footbridge, cross the Aire and a path ascends the slope in front onto the canal towpath at Hirst Lock. Go left for a short stroll back into Saltaire.

INDEX • *Walk number refers*

Aire, River	1,4,5,8,22,23,25
Alder Carr Wood	12
Baildon	24,25
Baildon Moor	24,25
Bank Newton	1
Beck Foot	22,23
Bingley	22,23
Bingley Moor	21
Black Moor	17,19
Bradley	7,8
Brow Moor	17
Carleton	4
Catstones Moor	20
Cononley	5
Cononley Ings	4,5
Cononley Lead Mine	5
Cowling	10
Crookrise Crag	2
Cross Hills	9
Cullingworth	19
Deer Gallows	3
Denholme	19
Doubler Stones	11
Druid's Altar	23
Earl Crag	10
Eastburn	9
Eastby	3
East Marton	1
East Morton	21
Eldwick	25
Embsay	2,3
Embsay Crag	2
Embsay Moor	2,3
Embsay Reservoir	2,3
Farnhill	8
Farnhill Moor	8
Five Rise Locks	22
Gargrave	1
Glusburn	5
Goitstock Wood	20
Goose Eye	13
Harden	20
Harden Moor	20
Hawksworth	24
Haworth	15,16,17
Haworth Moor	15,16
Hewenden	19
Keighley & Worth Valley Rly	16,17,18
Keighley Moor	13
Kildwick	8
Leeds & Liverpool Canal	1,7,8,11,12,22,25
Leeming	18
Lothersdale	6
Lower Laithe Res'r	16
Micklethwaite	21
Nab Hill	18
Newsholme Dean	13
Oakworth Moor	13
Oldfield	14
Oxenhope	17,18
Penistone Hill	15,16
Pinhaw Beacon	6
Ponden	14
Ponden Clough	14
Ramshaw	4
Riddlesden	12
Rombalds Moor	21
St Ives	23
Saltaire	22,25
Shipley Glen	25
Silsden	11
Skipton Moor	7
Slippery Ford	13
Snaygill	7
Stanbury	16
Stanbury Moor	14
Sunnydale	21
Sutton Clough	9
Sutton-in-Craven	9
Thimble Stones	21
Top Withins	15
Windgate Nick	11
Worth, River	14,16